The Church of
All Ages

The Church of All Ages

Generations Worshiping Together

Howard Vanderwell,
Editor

THE
ALBAN
INSTITUTE

Herndon, Virginia
www.alban.org

The Alban Institute
2121 Cooperative Way, Suite 100
Herndon, VA 20171

Cover design by Tobias Becker.

Library of Congress Cataloging-in-Publication Data

The church of all ages : generations worshiping together / Howard
Vanderwell, Editor.
    p. cm. — (The vital worship, healthy congregations series)
    Includes bibliographical references.
    ISBN-13: 978-1-56699-358-6
    1. Church. 2. Public worship. 3. Intergenerational relations—Reli-
gious aspects—Christianity. I. Vanderwell, Howard.
    BV600.3.C48 2007
    264—dc22
                2007035175

12 11 10 09 08   VG   1 2 3 4 5

I Was There to Hear Your Borning Cry

John Ylvisaker (b. 1937)

I was there to hear your borning cry,
I'll be there when you are old.
I rejoiced the day you were baptized
To see your life unfold.
I was there when you were but a child,
with a faith to suit you well;
in a blaze of light you wandered off
to find where demons dwell.

When you heard the wonder of the Word
I was there to cheer you on;
you were raised to praise the living Lord,
to whom you now belong.
If you find someone to share your time
and you join your hearts as one,
I'll be there to make your verses rhyme
from dusk till rising sun.

In the middle ages of your life,
not too old, no longer young,
I'll be there to guide you through the night,
complete what I've begun.
When the evening gently closes in
and you shut your weary eyes,
I'll be there as I have always been
with just one more surprise.

I was there to hear your borning cry,
I'll be there when you are old.
I rejoiced the day you were baptized
to see your life unfold.

Text: John Ylvisaker, b. 1937. Used by permission. Copyright © 1985
John Ylvisaker, P.O. Box 321, Waverly, Iowa 50677. (319) 352-4396.

Contents

Editor's Foreword

Healthy Congregations

Christianity is a "first-person plural" religion, where communal worship, service, fellowship, and learning are indispensable for grounding and forming individual faith. The strength of Christianity in North America depends on the presence of healthy, spiritually nourishing, well-functioning congregations. Congregations are the cradle of Christian faith, the communities in which children of all ages are supported, encouraged, and formed for lives of service. Congregations are the habitat in which the practices of the Christian life can flourish.

As living organisms, congregations are by definition in a constant state of change. Whether the changes are in membership, pastoral leadership, lay leadership, the needs of the community, or the broader culture, a crucial mark of healthy congregations is their ability to deal creatively and positively with change. The fast pace of change in contemporary culture, with its bias toward, not against, change only makes the challenge of negotiating change all the more pressing for congregations.

Vital Worship

At the center of many discussions about change in churches today is the topic of worship. This is not surprising, for worship is at the center of congregational life. To "go to church" means, for most members of congregations, "to go to worship." In *How Do We Worship?*, Mark Chaves begins his analysis with the simple assertion, "Worship is the most central and public activity engaged in by American religious congregations" (Alban Institute, 1999, p. 1). Worship styles are one of the most significant reasons that people choose to join a given congregation. Correspondingly, they are central to the identity of most congregations.

Worship is also central on a much deeper level. Worship is the locus of what several Christian traditions identify as the nourishing center of congregational life: preaching, common prayer, and the celebration of ordinances or sacraments. Significantly, what many traditions elevate to the status of "the means of grace" or even the "marks of the church" are essentially liturgical actions. Worship is central, most significantly, for theological reasons. Worship both reflects and shapes a community's faith. It expresses a congregation's view of God and enacts a congregation's relationship with God and each other.

We can identify several specific factors that contribute to spiritually vital worship and thereby strengthen congregational life.

- Congregations, and the leaders that serve them, need a shared vision for worship that is grounded in more than personal aesthetic tastes. This vision must draw on the deep theological resources of Scripture, the Christian tradition, and the unique history of the congregation.
- Congregational worship should be integrated with the whole life of the congregation. It can serve as the "source and summit" from which all the practices of the Christian life flow. Worship both reflects and shapes the life of the church in education, pastoral care, community service, fellowship, justice, hospitality, and every other aspect of church life.
- The best worship practices feature not only good worship "content," such as discerning sermons, honest prayers, creative artistic contributions, celebrative and meaningful rituals for baptism and the Lord's Supper. They also arise of out of good process, involving meaningful contributions from participants, thoughtful leadership, honest evaluation, and healthy communication among leaders.

Vital Worship, Healthy Congregations Series

The Vital Worship, Healthy Congregations Series is designed to reflect the kind of vibrant, creative energy and patient reflection that will promote worship that is both relevant and profound. It is designed to invite congregations to rediscover a common vision for worship, to sense how worship is related to all aspects of congregational life, and to imagine better ways of preparing both better "content" and better "process" related to the worship life of their own congregations.

It is important to note that strengthening congregational life through worship renewal is a delicate and challenging task precisely because of the uniqueness of each congregation. This book series is not designed to represent a single denomination, Christian tradition, or type of congregation. Nor is it designed to serve as arbiter of theological disputes about worship. Books in the series will note the significance of theological claims about worship, but they may, in fact, represent quite different theological visions from each other, or from our work at the Calvin Institute of Christian Worship. That is, the series is designed to call attention to instructive examples of congregational life and to explore these examples in ways that allow readers in very different communities to compare and contrast these examples with their own practice. The models described in any given book may for some readers be instructive as examples to follow. For others, a given example may remind them of something they are already doing well, or something they will choose not to follow because of theological commitments or community history.

The Church of All Ages: Generations Worshiping Together is an especially timely book that confronts one of the great tragedies of worship in the past several decades. For all kinds of reasons, many congregations have practiced a kind of generational segregation on Sunday morning. Some churches schedule Christian education sessions during worship so that families are split up during their hour at church. Some churches schedule different worship services for Boomers, Busters, and Gen X "audiences," tailoring

each service to the tastes and preferences of each generational cohort. The result of moves like these is a deepening division in the
body of Christ that is vexingly difficult to overcome. Nevertheless,
in our work at the Calvin Institute of Christian Worship we are
grateful for renewed interest in intergenerational practices. In fact,
the recent history of generational segregation seems to have generated quite a hunger for intergenerational community in which
children and older adults (and everyone in between) can be blessed
by the presence of each other. Though intergenerational worship
is hardly new, we're tempted to describe it as the new "cutting
edge" approach to worship, partly because of all the interest in the
topic we sense from churches from very different backgrounds,
and partly because we know that this is only kind of label that will
challenge innovation-loving churches to re-embrace intergenerational practices. In any case, we are heartened by renewed attention to this topic, and are eager to do anything to help churches of
all types experience worship with "old and young together" (see
Psalm 145:12).

By promoting encounters with instructive examples from various parts of the body of Christ, we pray that the volumes in the Vital Worship, Healthy Congregations series will help leaders make
good judgments about worship in their congregations and that, by
the power of God's Spirit, these congregations will flourish.

John D. Witvliet
Calvin Institute for Christian Worship

Foreword

Many of my students begin a semester referring to worship as "worship experience." I must confess that I am "allergic" to this phrase and always react negatively when students use it. In what I hope is a good-natured response, I describe my objections to the phrase, explaining that in worship the community of faith, more intentionally than at any other time, gathers in the presence of the triune God, the creator of heaven and earth. The full attention of all the faithful is on that Presence and on our proper orientation to "God, whom alone we worship and serve." The phrase "worship experience" indicates, perhaps subtly, that our attention has already shifted from worship's theocentric focus and instead is focused on ourselves—our own feelings, responses, actions, surroundings, likes, dislikes, etc. Often students are left almost speechless, unable to talk about worship at all unless they employ the now-banned phrase, and they are quick to ask what other words they might substitute. One of the words I usually suggest is "event." Worship is an "event," a set of circumstances, actions, and interactions that occur in a particular time and place and with a particular group of gathered participants. Of course it is an event that the participants experience, and that experience is spiritually, communally, and ethically formative. But experience is not really the point. The point is, according to Marva Dawn, to royally waste our time in the presence of the living God.

During the past couple of decades, liturgical experimentation, which comes from a variety of historical and cultural sources, has helped to inspire this focus on "worship experience." In the course of these experiments and in response to ever-increasing individualistic pressures from media-saturated, consumer-driven Western culture, worship planners and participants have been encouraged to take note of their own "experience" and to critique worship events based on that experience. Thomas Shattauer, in an address to the North American Academy of Liturgy in 2005, described this period of experimentation as a search for alternatives to what he defined as "conventional worship." Conventional worship can be described, according to Shattauer, as worship patterns that are generally accepted, customary, and focused on the life of the church as an institution. The church is understood to provide religious services of all kinds, including worship, and the recipients of those services are understood to be primarily individuals. Put more bluntly, the church is a franchise which provides religious services to its individual customers. Conventional worship tends to be clergy-centered, verbal/textual, limited in forms, and seeks to maintain the status quo. Liturgical reform movements have emerged with a variety of goals, says Shattauer, but all address the dominance of conventional worship. The wave of experimentation these reform movements have inspired has helped to break the almost universal hold of conventional worship on congregational practice. But one of the unintended consequences has been liturgical specialization, as particular styles of worship have been tailored to meet the expectations of particular demographic groups, especially generational cohorts. Thus congregations, and even whole denominations, have been fragmented, with old, young, and the in-between cut off from one another. Intergenerational worship has become "counter cultural" in a society where the segregation of age groups has become the norm.

With the publication of *The Church of All Ages: Generations Worshiping Together* and some of its companion volumes it appears that the fruits of this period of rich experimentation are ready to be harvested, sorted, and enjoyed by a great number of congregations. All of the contributors to this book, and especially its editor, Howard Vanderwell, take as their starting point the participation of all in the gathered assembly, as the whole community turns its attention toward the presence of the living God in their midst. They describe in vivid, winsome detail the gifts that each generation brings to the spiritual formation of all the others and describe how this deepening of communal attentiveness to the presence of

God strengthens the whole church in its faithfulness and mission. The book is a delightful combination of strong theological principles, insightful interdisciplinary theory, and practical suggestions for actually "binding the generations" within the congregation.

One of the most attractive features of this book is its grounding in real conversations with real worshipers, worship planners, and worship leaders. One has a sense of "overhearing" the conversations that took place at "The Church Together" conference, in addition to many voices from particular congregations. The authors explore "issues that are more important than style" in their emphasis on the "development of a healthy ethos or culture that is intergenerational through and through." Various chapters explore the multiple questions implicit in intergenerational worship and the biblical values that undergird it as a congregational norm. Each chapter concludes with discussion questions that make the book especially user-friendly. Many will be enlightened by Robert Keeley's exploration of worship and faith development. Descriptions of intergenerational culture by Gil Rendle and Darwin Glassford make a strong theoretical and practical case for initiating and strengthening this culture in the congregation. The heart of intergenerational congregational life is to be found in the telling of stories, say Jeff Barker and Tim Brown. They make this case convincingly, echoing Thomas Groome's assertion that Christians are a "story formed people" and describing the power to be found in biblical, personal, and homiletical storytelling. Brown and Barker offer a wide range of theoretically rich, yet practical suggestions for how the identity-forming power of biblical and personal narrative can become an integral part of the intergenerational culture of theocentric worship. The book is rounded out with descriptions of successful cultural change in actual congregations, along with many creative and usable ideas. The appendices are a treasure trove of additional resources that will whet the appetite of readers and get them started on cultural change in their own congregations.

In the foreword to one of the other volumes in this series, Paul Boers confesses that he had a number of years of pastoral experience under his belt before he realized the centrality and formative power of worship in congregational life. The writers of this timely addition to the Vital Worship, Healthy Congregations series make such confessions less likely. They are acutely aware of the "event-centered" quality of congregational worship and provide an enticing vision for intergenerational congregational culture that finds its center in worship. These writers invite us all to reconsider our recent liturgical experiments and to focus them on faithful, healthy, communal participation in declaring God's greatness.

Jane Rogers Vann
Union Theological Seminary and
Presbyterian School of Christian Education

Preface

This book has been born in the midst of quiet collisions that occur on multiple levels. Perhaps you have been feeling the impact of these collisions and couldn't quite identify what they were or where they were coming from.

When you look carefully at congregations today, you will recognize these collisions:

- within a society often marked by hands-off parenting in which busy two-career parents spend little time with their children, yet expect the church to focus more time and attention on them;
- between the desire of parents to have the weekend to be with their children and church programming that practices age segregation;
- between the realities of a small congregation with limited resources and the megachurch with seemingly unlimited resources and ministries for each age;
- between the presence of children in our pews and the increased number of seniors in the same pews;
- between those who desire formality and those who desire informality.

On another level, many of us have witnessed the collision between the church that advertises its ability to provide specialized ministries for every age on Sunday and the church that advertises itself as intergenerational. Behind so many of these clashes is the collision between different generations, expectations, and forms of communication.

This book comes out of those quiet and sometimes not-so-quiet collisions, because such circumstances seem to raise a question with new urgency: Should we try to hold the generations together when we worship? Is it possible? When I've visited churches in Michigan, New Jersey, Iowa, California, Tokyo, or Singapore, the question seems constant and transcendent of culture—rural, urban, Western, Latin American, or Asian.

I have seen, concurrent with all those collisions, a growth process of nearly 10 years in which this idea of intergenerational worship kept germinating in the minds of congregations. *Reformed Worship*, a quarterly journal with a 20-year history now, increasingly published editorials and articles that raised questions and explored the subject of intergenerational worship. In June 2005 an entire issue was devoted to this theme. The Calvin Institute of Christian Worship and the Chorister's Guild published *A Child Shall Lead: Children in Worship* in 1999 and broke new ground for exploring the active participation of children in worship. In 2005, a significant worship conference was held in Denver, Colorado. "The Church Together: Exploring Intergenerational Worship" drew worship planners from across North America. During this same period, the Calvin Institute of Christian Worship, which provides worship renewal grants to congregations and groups, found that a surprising number of them were intent on exploring intergenerational worship. For instance, a young congregation in California includes multigenerational participation in Scripture reading and involves all ages in memorizing Scripture together; a Covenant church in California aims to engage all generations in creative expression through the arts; a Korean congregation bridges the generations by providing multigenerational, bilingual weekly communion; and an African-American congregation in Michigan includes a young person on every committee.

All of these growing ideas crystallized into an excellent day of talking and thinking held on the campus of Calvin College in fall 2006. Forty participants from a variety of disciplines and denominational experiences gathered to spend an entire day talking together about the issues involved in intergenerational worship. Each brought his or her own experiences, good and bad. Each reflected a specific community and fellowship. Each reflected on the experimention that a home congregation is doing. Each agreed to work with others in wrestling with this subject that begs for greater attention. By the end of the day a rather clear picture had emerged of the material that you hold in your hands today. As we write this book, we owe a debt of gratitude to the participants for the contributions each has made. We are also grateful to the congregations that have nurtured us from childhood on, though they have often been unaware of how they served as laboratories for testing a variety of methods of ministering to all of us.

I should point out that some use the term "intergenerational" worship, while others prefer "multigenerational" worship. Throughout this book we have used both words and consider them to be roughly synonymous. Yet it appears to us that "multigenerational" speaks of multiple generations existing near each other and "intergenerational" implies that the multiple generations are engaged with each other. The latter is our ideal. You may want to discuss these terms and their implications in your planning group.

You will hear various voices in this book. We have drawn together a variety of writers to guide us. Some are pastors, some teachers, some worship planners, and some workers in specialized ministries; but all are deeply committed to the vitality of the local congregation and the nurturing of faith and spirit that takes place there. They will speak to us from their own experiences, locations, and concerns. After we listen to them all, we will be better able to guide our own communities. Each chapter begins with some introductory comments to aid the reader in understanding its place in the larger context of the book.

Chapter 1 helps us to see why this subject has suddenly appeared on the radar screen of churches. With increased longevity and diversity in our living, churches are facing new circumstances. Chapter 2 points to foundational biblical values that ought to shape our congregations. In chapter 3 we examine faith development in the lives of children and youth, and we discover some important guidelines for ministry. Chapter 4 helps us understand that we need a certain way of seeing. Generational cohorts are shaped by their experiences, and one cohort often sees things differently from another. Chapter 5 reminds us that becoming an intergenerational congregation in our worship cannot be done apart from the development of a healthy ethos or culture that is intergenerational through and through. Chapter 6 explores the powerful bond that can be created in a community through the telling of stories—Bible stories, personal stories, and congregational stories. In chapter 7 the sermon and preaching are in view. The task of making preaching accessible to all ages presents both challenges and opportunities; and both preachers and hearers will find this discussion helpful. In chapter 8 we learn from the research and experience of one large congregation whether a church must change its whole style of worship to remain intergenerational. From this congregation's experience we learn that there are issues more important than style. Chapter 9 takes us into the life of a congregation, shines the spotlight around, and helps us see many areas of worship in which the generations can successfully connect. In chapter 10 worship planners are the focus. Their work is broader and more complex when the congregation is intergenerational, and this chapter's ideas and guidelines were shaped in the laboratory of weekly worship planning. Appendixes are provided to make additional resources available.

We hope you will read through the entire book to see the big picture, and then go back and focus on the subjects and chapters that speak most clearly to your situation.

We have also included thirty-one "snapshots" from people in a variety of locations and experiences. Each gives us a glimpse of some event in the life of the church that reflects its intergenerational activities. These glimpses also illustrate the diversity of life and practice in the church today. As you read these brief narratives, imagine that you are paging through a scrapbook of photos of the body of Christ around the world. Looking at these snapshots will bring to life the contents of each chapter. We are deeply grateful to all these writers for making their perspectives available to us.

This material is written for the leaders, lay and clergy alike, who are given the large privilege and responsibility of shaping the ministry of the congregation. How these ministries are shaped will have a long-term impact on the faith life of our communities. All congregations experience more diversity with each passing year and face new questions. Yet we are able to draw on little research and data as a track record that evaluates the success or danger of new approaches. So wisdom and discernment must be developed.

It's obvious that the people in our congregation are not all the same. Age differences are most obvious. But adults in our pews continue to be diverse in their life circumstances. The children and youth in our congregations don't all have the same preferences. We also experience diversity in our abilities. Some are healthy; others live with physical, emotional, and mental disabilities. Some of those disabilities are associated with age, some with injury, and others with disease. When you stop to think of it, you realize that a congregation is a rich blend. The wonder and miracle is that these diverse people are bound together in a common faith and love—and given the privilege of being called the body of Christ in the world. Our task, therefore, in speaking about intergenerational worship is no small task.

This book aims not to prescribe exactly what you should do, but rather to raise the pertinent issues that should guide you as you design ministry for your congregation. There is no one way to do it. We do not propose easy answers or instant solutions. Diversity abounds: the generations have been formed differently, think differently, practice different methods of communication, and often desire widely different worship practices. We do not minimize these differences. Each of us will have to craft and design ministries and practices that reflect our own community, heritage, and history. For instance, you will not find us insisting that all children of all ages should be included in the worshiping community for the entire time of worship. Some children will be in the nursery. Some congregations will hold special children's worship times for the youngest children, and we leave to your discretion what the age guidelines should be.

We do, however, believe that each congregation should be discussing, among both clergy and laity, the specific approach it will take in such matters. The benefits of this book will be amply multiplied when it is used for discussion in a group. Each chapter includes questions and suggestions for discussions, and an appendix includes guidelines for the kinds of small groups in which this material can profitably be used.

Any undertaking such as this is the product of effective and Spirit-led collaboration. I am deeply grateful to three people who served as an editorial team and found it easy to exchange ideas, evaluations, and suggestions openly and candidly. Nathan Bierma, Norma deWaal Malefyt, and Robert Keeley, all on the staff of Calvin College, regularly contributed their valuable insights. The Calvin Institute of Christian Worship has been a community in which many helpful ideas were fostered and honed. Our director, John Witvliet, under whose supervision we work, has been encouraging and trusting. We are indebted to the Lilly Endowment, Inc., for its aid in our ministries and in making this project possible. The Alban Institute, whose publications have assisted us all in our ministries, now gives us the privilege of aiding others, and we give thanks for them. Our Alban editors, Beth Gaede and Jean Caffey Lyles, have been gifts to us all along the way. Their expertise, advice, encouragement, and understanding have made this process enjoyable and satisfying.

While there is no greater privilege than the Christian practice of worshiping God, we believe there is no better way to do that than as an intergenerational community in which all are important, all celebrate, all communicate, and all encourage and nurture the faith of the others. As pilgrims on a journey, we travel together.

Howard Vanderwell

CHAPTER 1

A New Issue for a New Day

Howard Vanderwell

Each day brings new opportunities—and new questions as well. The question of intergenerational worship is a new one for our day. Before we address other aspects of this issue, we first need to understand why the issue is cropping up now.

A couple of generations ago this book would never have been written. And if we had written it, no one would have published it. Nor would you have read it. Intergenerational worship was a nonissue. Few thought of it. Nobody talked about it.

But today the issue of intergenerational worship is on the front burner. The importance of this issue will only increase in the years ahead as congregations grapple with the development of effective ministries. The lively interest we have detected as this book was proposed and developed confirms our conviction that intergenerational worship is an issue whose day has come.

A Robust Issue

A Google search of "intergenerational worship" and "family worship" will reveal thousands of pages of material. Many congregations are obviously eager to promote themselves as places where intergenerational worship takes place. They have learned that this mark of their ministry carries weight with those who are looking for a place to worship. For some congregations, intergenerational worship means that children and youth are drawn into worship on several carefully planned occasions during the year. For others it means that children are welcomed into worship for the early part of the service before they are dismissed to their age-appropriate activities. Others declare that worshipers of all ages are welcome at their communion services. And still others tell us that youth-planned worship services are provided according to a regular schedule. The variety is great, but the common thread is that congregations are eager to portray themselves as "intergenerational." Rare, however, is the congregation that says its worship is planned to welcome all generations consistently on a weekly basis.

When my colleagues and I lead conferences on worship in congregations both in North America and elsewhere, we find certain issues and questions consistently coming up in discussion. The regularity with which such matters arise becomes a window through which we are able to observe the issues that are making worship planners and leaders nervous today. We regularly encounter such questions as these: How can we increase collaboration among worship planners? How can the use of visuals and art aid our worship life? Is it possible to prevent, or at least contain, conflict over worship issues? What style of music should we embrace? And discussions almost always include this question: Can worship be intentionally intergenerational, and if so, how?

The issue is here to stay. Several factors explain why this matter of intergenerational worship has risen to the top.

Increasing Longevity

Simply put, people are living longer today, and so the worshiping congregation includes more seniors than it did a generation ago. Since it includes more seniors, the age difference between people in the same pew is greater than it might have been in earlier years. Circumstances like that creep upon us slowly and almost unnoticed until finally we realize that we have a different culture to deal with.

Michael Stein, a financial advisor who specializes in preparations for retirement, tells us that "Since 1990, the life expectancy of older Americans has increased by 52% and the trend seems to be accelerating."[1] He cites findings from "Vital Statistics of the United States," a report prepared annually by a branch of the U.S. Department of Health and Human Services that reveals how life expectancy has changed. In 1900 life expectancy was 50 years; in 1925 it was 57 years; by 1950 it had reached 68 years; in 1975 it was 72 years; and by 2000 the average life expectancy had become approximately 76 years.

Kathleen Fischer, a counselor and spiritual director who writes about the relationship of spirituality and aging, opens her book *Winter Grace* by showing us the impact of this trend on our communities. "In 1990 there were 32 million persons in the United States aged 65 and over. By the year 2020, the number will rise to 52 million and by 2030 it will include more than one in every five Americans [about 70 million]."[2]

In my own experience, three of my four grandparents died before my fifth birthday. I have no knowledge of them except what has come through family photos and shared memories. I don't recall encounters with them, and I surely don't recall ever sitting next to them in church. My grandfather was a pastor who baptized me as an infant. I know of that event because I have been told the story, but I have no memory of it. On the other hand, when my first three grandchildren were born and baptized, my parents were still living, and we took family photos of four generations together. And even today I can attend worship while sitting in the same pew with my children, who are in their 40s, and my grandchildren, who range in age from 6 to 19.

We can easily understand how this change affects our congregations. As the number of older adults grows, the congregation faces new challenges and opportunities for ministry. Fellowship ministries are needed for those who often are alone. Caregiving ministries are called for as more seniors experience health-related needs. But service opportunities can also be expanded, for we find that many healthy seniors are eager to volunteer for service projects. Worship is also affected. Not only will there be more seniors in worship, but also the age differentiation in a pew is likely to be much larger than it was a generation ago. As a pastor, I have served a congregation in which I often had the privilege of seeing four-generation families sitting near each other in worship. Often an age range of 80 years existed in the same pew.

Our pews have become intergenerational in a way that would have been unthinkable some years ago. Longevity has created a new day in the worshiping congregation.

Diversity among Generations

Yet even as we live longer and multiple generations sit in the same pew, the experiences that shape us are more diverse than ever. For my grandchildren, understanding and living with technology is second nature, while I fumble through instruction booklets, not even understanding the terminology. I watch TV commercials that I don't understand, and I'm told that happens because they are targeting a generation other than my own. There were differences in lifestyle that I had to consider when I was an adolescent, but they were less severe than the lifestyle issues between the generations today. Our world was small; our concerns were local. Today adolescents live in an international world. Our vocabularies are very different. Our communicating, thinking, reacting, and feeling are different.

I remember a Sunday evening in 1969 when my father, then slightly over 60 years old, was in our home as we watched the televised reports of Apollo 11 and its moon landing. Neil Armstrong walked on the moon that night, the first in human history to do so. My father watched quietly. Then, with a tear in his eye, he expressed his awe not just at this event, but at the pace of change in our world. He went on to explain that he could recall the first time he saw an automobile drive through town, the first time he saw a steam engine puff into our city, and the first time an airplane landed at our local airport. And then he actually flew in a jet aircraft. "And now," he said, choking up, "I not only watch television and hear about traveling to the moon, but I see it as it actually happens! I just can't imagine it all!" He had captured not only the increasingly rapid pace of change, but also how differently the generations were being shaped by this rate of change. A friend tells of a conversation with her 78-year-old mother, who often comments, "Given all the changes I've seen in the past 20 years, I can't

The Same Stories

Norma de Waal Malefyt

I remember well the times when we sat with our first infant son and read Bible stories to him. We were pleased to be parents, and we wanted to start early in training him well. So we had a Bible storybook that was "his."

Sometimes on the couch and sometimes at the table, we would read the stories that were so familiar to us, and that needed to be planted in his heart. He learned to listen well and to love the stories—and the pictures that went along with them. We learned to treasure the time of reading them.

That Bible storybook became a familiar fixture in our home, and reading from it a regular practice in our home as our family grew to include more children.

Now that little boy has become a father. He carries for his young daughter the same deep desire for her to know and love God that we carried for him when he was a child. And those stories of God's actions shaped both our faith and his.

Imagine my delight last month when I spent time at our son's home and saw that he was reading to my granddaughter from a new edition of the very same Bible storybook we had used. What a precious picture! Little Grace listens as attentively as her father did to the same stories from the same book—30 years later. The stories, the book, and the practice are timeless.

even imagine what will happen in the next 20—and I'm not sure I want to be here to see it!"

We can try to identify the resulting diversity among the folk in our communities and congregations in a variety of ways. Yet we must be cautious about magnifying the differences. Perhaps the simplest and most obvious method, the one with which most people begin, is to note that people are at different chapters in life chronologically—some are children, some are adolescents, some have entered early adulthood, others are middle-aged, and some are seniors. Sometimes but not always, this means that some are grandparents, some are parents, some are grandchildren, and still others are great-grandchildren.

Sociologists point to each generation's time of birth as a baseline because the economic, social, and political events of the day will have shaped each one differently. Though a variety of categories may be used, the generations living today are sometimes referred to the "matures," the "baby boomers," the "gen Xers," and the "millenials."[3] Each, we are told, has its own value system and its own manner of communicating and responding.

Gil Rendle, a former senior consultant with the Alban Institute, has provided another helpful way for us to view our congregations. He looks at tenure of membership in the congregation and notes that some are long-tenured members (more than 20 years), some are mid-tenured (between 10 and 20 years), and others are short-tenured (less than 10 years). Rendle explains that each of these groups will have a different way of responding to change in the congregation and dealing with issues, and will likely possess somewhat different value systems.[4]

Craig Barnes, formerly pastor of the National Presbyterian Church in Washington, D.C., and now professor of leadership and ministry at Pittsburgh Theological Seminary, encourages us to look at the generations from another perspective. There is a longing for home in each soul, Barnes says, and this longing is reflected in our journeys of life. In his insightful book *Searching for Home*,[5] he speaks of the Settlers, who arrive in an area, sink their roots in and never consider moving away; the Exiles, who have grown up in a certain area but have moved to another area for work, education, or marriage, yet always consider their original location "home" and will return frequently; and finally, the Nomads, people who are on the move and consider no place "home" except where they happen to be at the time. Each of these groups thinks, reacts, and communicates from a different value system.

In some immigrating cultures we find still another expression of differentiation. In Korean culture in the United States, members of the first generation to immigrate are often called the "Ones"— those who received all their education and formation for life in their country of origin and often hold to their native language and many native customs. Second-generation members are called

"Twos"—those who received their education in the new land and are shaped largely by American values and will often adopt American lifestyles and language. The generation in between is often called "1.5" because its members straddle both cultures and attempt to bridge the customs of their native land and those of their new land. Attending a conference at a large Korean church in Los Angeles, I was surprised to hear one of the presenters caution us at the opening of his lecture that we must remember he is a 1.5 to understand how he approaches his subject.

Given the escalating longevity and growing diversity among the generations within congregations, worship leaders face an increasingly complex task. Both factors mean that worshiping congregations are likely less homogeneous than they might have been some time ago.

And along the way two other factors have entered in. First, the church of the past 25 or 30 years has taken Jesus's command to welcome children more seriously than before. Children are no longer expected only to be silent and to observe. As a society we now recognize the rights of children—rights that were not considered for centuries before. So congregations and pastors are expected to recognize the children, include the children in their references and illustrations, and provide "sermons" for children. The worship service will likely include a children's choir. Secondly, youth and young adults can now more readily leave the church than before. We are a much more mobile society, and the stigma of a 20-year-old's no longer attending church has lost nearly all its power. Since young people can and do leave church, churches have started thinking more about pleasing and keeping them.

What is a leader to do? Particularly, what must worship planners do? How can we hold multiple generations together? Some even ask: Should we try?

Ministry Diversity

Often practices in ministry develop in response to specific situations yet carry a significance and impact greater than originally thought or intended.

Casey's New Family

Carol Rottman

When Casey Vanden Bosch could no longer drive because of poor eyesight, she decided to retire from her many volunteer jobs in Fort Collins, Colorado, and to move near two daughters in Michigan. Immanuel Church had been her church home for 18 years, since she was widowed. Could she find another "home" at 89? Her requirements were straightforward: not too formal, but with more organ than drums; preaching she could hear and understand; and people who wanted to know her first as Casey, not as someone's mother.

She found her new home within the congregation at Eastern Avenue Church, in a pew near the front with family. During the bustling coffee hour after the service she sat in an easy chair on the side. Someone always delivered a half-cup of decaf, with a little cream and a little sugar, and pulled up a few chairs beside her. Soon the silver-haired lady was telling fascinating stories to strangers, slipping mints to kids, or holding a newly baptized baby. One member always drove her to church; afterward she went to her daughter's home for Sunday dinner, often accompanied by other folk who would soon count Casey as a friend.

Three years later, Casey's newfound family gathered at Eastern Avenue Church to say their final good-byes. On Sundays thereafter, they passed her empty chair with sadness but thanked God for the smiles and the stories Casey had shared when she became their adopted great-grandmother, worshiping among them until God called her home.

The matters cited above have led many congregations to rethink their programs of ministry in almost every respect. Youth ministries, education ministries, pastoral ministries, service ministries, and discipleship and outreach ministries have all gone through fundamental re-examination and change in the past 25 years.

As we would expect, worship ministry experienced the same re-examination and change. For a time churches tried to ignore the differences of the generations and assumed it was a matter they need not address. But gradually, and without much fanfare, changes began to take place in response to these new circumstances. Church leaders sensed that worshipers' expectations were changing, and they had to respond. Gradually the children's sermon made its way into Sunday-morning worship. Pastors gave the children personal attention, their age group became visible during worship, and the children felt "included." Parents were delighted to see their children go forward to talk with the pastor, and the congregation found it profitable to listen in as pastors devised clever methods of communicating with children.

The music ministry also began to pay more attention to children and their involvement. Children's choirs became popular, and the congregation (especially parents) loved it when the children's choir was included in worship. Children's music ensembles of various kinds appeared. Though the congregation found it difficult to resist thinking of these as cute performances, they strongly approved of including such groups in worship leadership.

The next wave of approach to this issue saw the children dismissed midway through the worship service so that they could attend classes and activities designed for their own age level. Some congregations accomplished this maneuver by moving the time of children's Sunday school so that it met simultaneously with worship. Others planned age-appropriate worship activities for children. Some called it children's church or worship center. Though it was often claimed that the intent was that children would learn to worship better if the event was structured and conducted at their learning level, many parents nonetheless were relieved and pleased. They found their children to be a distraction in worship and the kids "couldn't understand anything anyway." As part of this pattern, congregations often diversified their offerings for children's worship. Whereas one congregation might offer only a nursery for the infants, others dismissed preschoolers or kindergartners for children's classes; others extended the age through the second, third, or even fourth grade. At some churches parents could drop off their children at a separate building on their way into worship. The net result was that often young children were gone from the worship service before the pastor began the sermon.

Concurrent with both of these developments was the increasing sound of voices recommending niche programming for the worship life of the church. It's impossible to satisfy everyone, they contended, so it's best to separate kids and grown-ups and to plan worship that will minister more effectively to each. As part of this thinking, we were told that "seekers" would not be satisfied in the church's traditional worship, so "seeker worship"—worship that was, if not seeker-driven, at least seeker-friendly—would be necessary. Similarly, we were led to believe that because of differing expectations, it probably would be better to have both a "traditional" and a "contemporary" worship service on Sunday morning.

So churches began to show more and more diversity on Sunday morning. And worshipers learned to shop and select churches on the basis of what was available for their children.

At the same time, many smaller congregations were left in a cloud of doubt about themselves. Since the average church in America has fewer than 100 members, most of these congregations do not have the resources to implement any of the types of ministries cited above. What should they do? Are they failing in ministry if they can't keep up with the larger congregations? Should they feel they have less validity? Our contacts with churches reveal that many of them are wrestling with a fear that their small size and limited resources doom them to a lower level of effectiveness.

Gradually, it became clear that it might be wise to include all ages in the worshiping congregation. The idea of intergenerational worship was an issue whose time had come. We needed to face the matter, ask the hard questions, and evaluate all these attempts in the light of principles that would guide us all.

And the congregation seemed the logical place to study the matter. The efforts of many churches during the past generation have given ample opportunity to study the results, or lack of results, in these communities. The congregation is the dominant location of all religious gatherings in our society. On any given Sunday, approximately 350,000 congregations of all sorts gather, with some 75 million in attendance. Where else in our society do we have such a strategic location to examine and foster the relationships of generations?

Clarifying the Term

So far we've been using the term "intergenerational" without clearly defining it. Since this concept can mean many things, we should examine it more closely.

To many, any conversation about intergenerational worship is met with, "Yes, we need to include our children and youth more," or "We ought to find a way for our kids to feel more at home in our worship services." However, in this book we are using this term in a much more comprehensive way.

"Intergenerational worship" is worship in which people of every age are understood to be equally important.

Each generation has the same significance before the face of God and in the worshiping congregation. Each and all are made in the image of God. Each and all have worth. It is only a half-truth to make statements like "Our children and youth are the church of the future," or "Our seniors are the church of the past." Each and all are the church of *now*.

When I stand before a congregation at worship, I note that it is an intergenerational body when I see and hear:

- Jacob, an active third grader, writing on his children's bulletin.
- Grace, a vivacious high-school freshman, singing in the adult choir.
- Rich and Laura and their children, a busy young family seated together in the pew.
- Lou, well into his 80s, singing heartily.
- Jason, a gifted college student, taking sermon notes while sitting next to his father.
- Sue and Mary, mother and daughter, worshiping together, while five-year-old Luke moves back and forth between Mom and Grandma.

- Harriet, an active and vibrant 69-year-old, admitting that it's a lot harder walking the Christian life at her age than she had anticipated.
- Sue preaching a sermon that engages a teenager and a 52-year-old alike with an explanation of God's promises for all generations.
- Harold providing a sermon outline that adults can follow, and another for middle-schoolers.
- Natalie and her eighth-grade daughter, Amy, participating in the same praise team.

When a worshiping congregation considers all ages equally important, listens to the needs of all, engages all, and brings them all into an encounter with God, it will be successfully intergenerational. That is our goal.

Can It Be Done?

The complexity of this task is rather obvious. When we suggest that we aim for intergenerational worship, we are setting a high goal. Is it out of reach, or is it feasible?

While we may hear many generalizations, we must be wary of stereotypes that fail to do justice to the uniqueness of each generation. In the same way, each congregation has its own individuality. Congregations, even of the same denomination within the same community, differ from one another in their personalities, as well as in their unspoken and unwritten norms.

So we readily acknowledge that there are no simple answers in the search to be successfully intergenerational in our worship. Differing viewpoints will appear. A variety of practices will develop. And in this book you will not hear us say, "This is the only way to do it if you want to do it well." We will not claim that we have the final word from the Lord on the matter.

Instead, we aim to identify the problems that our congregations face at this point in history. We aim to raise the issues to a higher level of awareness. We aim to help you think carefully through all the implications involved. And we aim to foster dia-

Five Generations

Howard Vanderwell

The elders at Faith Church always gather for prayer before worship begins. It is a meaningful time of asking God's Spirit to come down and richly bless the worship service.

But this time one of the elders had an announcement that put a lot of things in a bigger picture. "Yesterday," he said, "there was an important birth in the life of our congregation." All births are important, we all thought. But then he went on to say, "James Edward was born yesterday morning to James and Heather, and the important part of this is that there are now five generations of this family in our congregation. James Edward is the son of James Albert, who is the son of James Neal, who is the son of Menno, who is the son of Peter!"

We all found smiles crossing our faces. We could picture the generational line of this family right here in this congregation.

I can imagine baptism morning: five generations sitting there together! Great-great-grandparents sitting in the front row, and all their family with them!

As I stood before the congregation that morning, I saw them in a different light. I took special note of the grandparents and the little children and all ages in between. How beautiful! I wondered how many congregations could picture five generations sitting together. And I wondered how it would feel to sit with my great-great-grandchildren in church.

logue within your congregation and among worship leaders across the land.

You will hear multiple voices in this book. Each will speak from personal experience and careful research, having listened to many others. And each will speak with a deep love for the church of Christ and all its members.

But at the end of the day, you will discover that there is no one simple solution to a complex set of circumstances. You will be left to consult and collaborate with other local leaders to assess your congregation, evaluate your past attempts, learn from others, and design new possibilities.

Jackson W. Carroll and Wade Clark Roof, a professor emeritus of religion and society at Duke University Divinity School and a professor of religion and society at the University of California, Santa Barbara, respectively, studied a variety of representative congregations and campus ministries in both North Carolina and southern California. They focused on how different religious communities confront the tension between generations. They presented their observations in their well-documented study *Bridging Divided Worlds*.[6] They explain that nearly all attempts to address this matter fit into one of three approaches to the matter. The "inherited-tradition congregation" seeks to conserve what the congregation has inherited from its denominational tradition, the congregation's own experience, and its ethnic heritage. Members of the congregation practice what they have inherited, rather than work at adapting it to new circumstances. The "blended congregation" is one where a conscious effort is made to appeal to all the generations it encompasses. It values traditional practices but adapts them with sensitivity to contemporary culture, though not without some tension and conflict. The "generation-specific congregation" is designed to address the cultural characteristics and needs of a particular generation. In its focus on one generation, its members and leaders feel no obligation to consider other generations. However, these latter tend to be new ministries that began without many inherited customs.

The authors indicate that, while all three inherently have unique strengths, weaknesses, and potential conflicts, the second—the blended congregation—has the greatest potential for success in becoming genuinely intergenerational. Even here, however, the emergence of tension and conflict is inevitable.

In this book, you will find us generally following the pattern of the "blended congregations" of which Carroll and Roof speak. To value our traditions without concern for current adaptation will leave a congregation unfit to reach all generations now and in the future. To focus on a particular generation with no obligation to consider others fails to do justice to the nature of the Christian church as the body of Christ, including old and young alike. And so we will aim to find our way among the efforts of blending, as Carroll and Roof identify it.

All in all, it's a new issue for a new day, an issue whose time has come.

Discussion Questions

1. Recall some of the attempts your congregation has made to be more intergenerational. What were they? Do you consider them to have been well thought through? Were they helpful?

2. Which insights on intergenerational worship cited in this chapter are most helpful in trying to understand your congregation?

3. Imagine you are a stranger who steps into worship with your congregation. What things do you think you would see that give glimpses of successful intergenerational worship?

4. How has the increase of longevity affected your congregation? What percentage of worshipers is in each age category? How has that changed in the past 10 years?

5. Which age group do you think feels most overlooked or left out in your congregation?

Howard Vanderwell is currently a resource development specialist for pastoral leadership at the Calvin Institute of Christian Worship and adjunct professor of Worship at Calvin Theological Seminary. He previously served in the pastorate for 40 years. He is co-author of Designing Worship Together: Models and Strategies for Worship Planning.

CHAPTER 2

Biblical Values to Shape the Congregation

Howard Vanderwell

It will become clear throughout this book that effective intergenerational worship requires careful and committed effort on the part of those who lead and plan worship. This chapter explores the biblical reasons for taking on such a complex task. The Bible speaks of values that ought to shape us as congregations. This chapter identifies those values for us to consider.

One Saturday a colleague and I were leading a workshop on intergenerational worship for a group of churches. The planning committee had suggested this topic. All the participants seemed attentive. Their questions and responses indicated a high level of interest. It was encouraging to us that they were dealing with questions and issues they had not identified before.

But after the morning session, several of the participants came up to talk. They seemed troubled. "What you say sounds so good and so true," one of them said. "But it just seems like such a huge task. I don't really know if we could make the worship in our church truly intergenerational. There's just too much to do! This is going to be too hard, I'm afraid."

We talked for a short while, and I agreed that this would, indeed, be a large task. It would be difficult. I didn't want to downplay that at all. Yet at the same time, I didn't want them to give up on an important part of ministry. At times our tasks are demanding yet so valuable that we must draw on a healthy motivation to give it our best. Otherwise, we will be tempted to give up the work when it gets to be more difficult than we first thought.

Jesus felt he had to address that very issue one day. When someone wants to build a tower, he asked, "Which of you . . . does not first sit down and estimate the cost, to see whether he has enough to complete it?" Otherwise he may not be able to finish, and others will ridicule him because he couldn't finish what he began (see Luke 14:28-31). Then, to reinforce his point, Jesus repeated it, illustrating it with the scenario about a king who was planning to go to war but had not calculated the cost. He consequently was forced to negotiate a settlement midway through.

Some may consider this issue of intergenerational worship one not worth pursuing. It will be too complex to minister successfully to all ages, and the cost will be too high, they say. I've heard the voices, and so have you.

"Why should we try to get a five-year-old to sing with us?"

"A middle-schooler needs to be active, not sitting still listening, and there's no way we can provide for activity in a worship service."

"An adolescent needs visuals with constantly changing images, and will never become engaged in our kind of worship."

"The 30-somethings and the 70-somethings think and feel so differently and face such different issues; how can one sermon ever expect to connect with both age groups?"

"Aren't we handing a pastor and worship planners an impossible task?"

And so some say, "How much easier it will be if we just let them all worship with their peers on their own level and in their own way!" After all, our whole society is increasingly structured that way. We separate the generations in school and in community activities. Church education separates the ages for the most part. Advertisers design their commercials to focus on one group, knowing they cannot reach all generations at once. Even a large mall near our home is clearly designed for a certain slice of the age spectrum. Why shouldn't worship be that way too?

Biblical Principles to Consider

Is intergenerational worship a lost cause? No. Will it be a tough task? Yes. But there are good reasons to take on a task so complex.

This chapter aims to spell out five good reasons in the form of biblical principles that shape the Christian congregation and together make the case for intergenerational worship. Though none of these considerations could individually carry the weight of the argument for intergenerational worship, their cumulative impact is convincing.

The Unity of the Church

Much has been said about the unity of the church—its importance, its maintenance, its brokenness, and all our efforts to protect it. The Bible makes clear that unity is a gift of Christ to his church. He provides it, and so the Bible speaks of the unity of the church as something that *is*. In his high-priestly prayer we are given the privilege of listening in on the conversation between Jesus and his Father. He prays, "The glory that you have given me I have given them, so that they may be one, as we are one, I in them and you in me, that they may become completely one, so that the world may know that you have sent me and have loved them even as you have loved me" (John 17:22-23). And Paul writes to the Ephesians, "There *is* one body and one Spirit, just as you were called to the one hope of your calling, one Lord, one faith, one baptism, one God and Father of all, who is above all and through all and in all" (Ephes. 4:4-6, italics added). Notice the number of times that the words "all" and "one" appear together in the same sentence. In his classic metaphor to the Corinthians Paul explains that the unity of the church is characterized by wide diversity, and he uses the human body to illustrate his point. "For just as the body is one and has many members, and all the members of the body, though many, are one body, so it is with Christ. For in the one Spirit we were all baptized into one body—Jews or Greeks, slaves or free—and we were all made to drink of one Spirit" (1 Cor. 12:12). Similarly, Paul says in Romans 12:5, "we, who are many, are one body in Christ, and individually we are members one of another."

But the unique character of this unity is found in the fact that the members of this unified body are so different. Some are Jews with a long history of relationships with God; some are Gentiles who have long been considered outside God's love. Some serve in visible roles like a hand or a foot or a mouth; others serve in less visible roles like the parts of our physical body we consider more private. Some are strong; some are weak. Some are slaves; some are free. Some are children; some are adults.

On the one hand, the Bible tells us that this unity *is*. It exists because Christ has bound us all together. Yet on the other hand, it must be preserved because it can be fragile and easily lost. So the apostle exhorts us to make "every effort to maintain the unity of the Spirit in the bond of peace" (Ephes. 4:3). Therefore, it is impossible to address generational differences in the life of the church without giving careful consideration to both sides of this teaching—unity *is*, and unity needs to be maintained.

The Pattern of Worship

Students of early Christian worship have often wished that both Scripture and early historical accounts had given us more detailed accounts of early worship practices. Having more information would be helpful. On the other hand, we must admit that having more complete information might make us feel constrained to follow only the first Christians' pattern and limit our ability to adapt worship practices to our current needs. Yet though we are not given details, we have been given enough glimpses of early worship life to make a number of principles clear. One such principle in that God's people have always included all ages in their worship.

When God delivered the Hebrews from the bondage of slavery in Egypt, he instructed them to observe the Passover regularly as a reminder of his gracious deliverance (see Exod. 12). This ceremony was intended to be a constant reminder to the Hebrews that God had mightily delivered them with his gracious hand. God even gave them specific instructions on how to observe it—when to schedule it, the lamb to be selected, the use of the lamb's blood, the food to be prepared, and the clothing to wear. God's intent was that this celebration should be permanent among the Hebrews and that it should include a retelling of the Exodus story throughout their history. Therefore, it is significant that the children of the Hebrew family are expected not only to be present, but to partici-

Whose Party Is This Anyway?

Robert Nordling

A number of years ago, our son was invited to his friend's fourth birthday party. Bursting with anticipation, he was most excited about finding his friend a birthday present. Finally the great day arrived. We drove our son over to the little boy's house, took him to the door, met the hosts, and then said good-bye with assurances that we would return to pick up our son right after the party was over.

We arrived back a few hours later and quickly saw a much less enthusiastic boy get into the car. We could tell right away that something was up. We asked, "How was the party, son?"

"Oh, all right, . . . I guess."

"Why? What's the matter? Didn't you have a good time?"

"Yes . . . but I didn't get any presents!"

"But . . . er, son, it wasn't your party."

Unconvinced and unconsoled, he sat for the rest of the ride home generally depressed by the seeming injustice of it all.

As we rode home, it seemed that the Lord spoke to me and said, "Too often, that's just like my church in worship—so quick to look for gifts and blessings, and so unready to bring something to give away."

Ouch!

pate by asking the probing question: "What do you mean by this observance?" (Exod. 12:26, 13:14). This question from children would be the trigger throughout the generations for a recounting of their history. Whenever the child would ask the question, the family would hear the whole story again. Even today, a young Jewish child asks probing questions at the family's Seder meal about why this night is different from all other nights.

At numerous times in Israel's history, we are able to observe worship life when the people of Israel are experiencing a renewal of God's covenant. In many of these instances the Scriptures clearly show that all generations are present. We might expect that only the father of the family or the elders of the nation would be present, but references show that these times of worship are intergenerational events.

In Deuteronomy, while Moses was leading Israel through the wilderness, he called the people to renew their covenant with God in a time of worship, and Moses described the intergenerational nature of the congregation—"the leaders of your tribes, your elders, and your officials, all the men of Israel, your children, your women, and the aliens who are in your camp" (Deut. 29:10-11). When Israel had crossed the Jordan under the leadership of Joshua, Moses' successor, the people carried out the conquest of Jericho but then experienced a humiliating defeat in battle in punishment for one warrior's sin. So once again they were called together for a renewal of the covenant, and Joshua led them. "There was not a word of all that Moses commanded that Joshua did not read before all the assembly of Israel, and the women, and the little ones, and the aliens who resided among then" (Josh. 8:35).

Much later, after King Solomon had built the Temple for Israel in Jerusalem, we find similar worship events involving all generations. Jehoshaphat led them in renewal, and "all Judah stood before the Lord, with their little ones, their wives, and their children" (2 Chron. 20:13). When Nehemiah led them in rebuilding the wall of Jersualem after their return from exile, Ezra called them together as an intergenerational congregation. He read the book of the law to them before the Water Gate from early morning until midday "in the presence of the men and the women and those who could understand" (Neh. 8:3). When we collect all these valuable glimpses, we are not surprised that Psalm 148 should exclaim: "Young men and women alike, old and young together! Let them praise the name of the Lord, for his name alone is exalted; his glory is above earth and heaven" (Ps. 148:12-13). This is our story just as it was theirs, and we are living it out in our communities each week.

A Covenant Community

Another thing we notice is how regularly we are reminded of God's interest in all generations. Early in biblical history, in Genesis 17,

God said to Abraham, "I will establish my covenant between me and you, and your offspring after you throughout their generations, for an everlasting covenant, to be God to you and to your offspring after you" (Gen. 17:7). And then God provided circumcision for the male offspring as a sign of their belonging to this community. What we see here is a glimpse into the nature of God and his method of working. God does not start from scratch with each new generation but deals with parents and their offspring as a unit.

Many churches readily use the word "covenant" in their theology to express this value. They often practice infant baptism as an expression of what they call their covenant theology. Through baptism, they believe, even infants are received into the Christian church. In other churches the word "covenant" rarely appears, and only adults are baptized. Yet when these churches "dedicate" their children, they profess that God has a unique and special interest in them. In nearly all congregations, the underlying belief is that God is interested in all ages from one generation to the next and that God does not start from the beginning with each new generation as though there had been no vested interest in the family before this time. God speaks about working from "generation to generation," expressing a special interest in both parents and their children.

God's dealings with the generations are regularly reinforced in the rest of the Bible, particularly the New Testament. Jesus paid special attention to children, and he became indignant when others tried to dissuade him from giving his blessing to little ones (see Mark 10:13-16). At Pentecost, when the Holy Spirit was poured out on the Christian church, many in Jerusalem were astonished and confused, so Peter explained the significance of this event in his sermon. Then he concluded his sermon by claiming this gift of the Holy Spirit as available to all who would believe in the name of Jesus Christ. And he went on to say, "For the promise is for you, *for your children,* and for all who are far away, everyone whom the Lord our God calls to him" (Acts 2:38-39; italics added). In the next few years "household" baptisms occurred in the early Christian church as evidence of believers' conviction that God deals with people as a family unit (Acts 16:15, 31-34 and 1 Cor. 1:16).

In addition, we find the Scriptures often affirming that the work of the Holy Spirit can be expected in believers of all ages, adults and children. Joel the prophet claimed that God would be pouring out his Spirit "on all flesh; your sons and your daughters . . . your old men . . . and your young men. . . . even on the male and female slaves" (Joel 2:28-29). Obviously, the work of God's Holy Spirit is age-inclusive, an insight into the heart of God himself. These references help us to understand the significance of the phrase "all generations." I recently examined my *Young's Analytical Concordance to the Bible* and found that the phrase "in/throughout/among the generations" appears more than 90 times. The church God calls together is a community in which all ages are valued.

Formation of Character

Chapter 3 of this book addresses spiritual formation. The formation of our faith and character is a complex process, one never fully completed during our days on this earth, and many influences shape it. Yet while complex, it is important; it determines in large part our qualifications for effective and productive service in the kingdom of God.

What interests us here is that God does not give us a fully formed character. Nor does God form our character as a sovereign act all alone, or expect us to form our own character unilaterally. The formation of our character in the economy of God is a community event. We aid each other in such formation. God acts on us through others. And, in particular, the working together of the generations is a necessary component of healthy formation. Each age learns from another. The young learn from the old, who have become seasoned by the experiences of life. And the old learn from the young in their new exploration of life. Everywhere in this process, the assumption is that the generations are cooperating with each other. And since the formation of faith and character is an essential concern of the Christian church, we should aim to keep the generations engaged with each other, both in ministry activities and in corporate worship.

We have already seen how the parents and children talk together during the Passover celebration. Children ask what the event means, and parents explain the Exodus, so that the young learn and the older family members don't forget. Moses directly addresses this need:

> Keep these words that I am commanding you today in your heart. Recite them to your children and talk about them when you are at home and when you are away, when you lie down and when you rise. Bind them as a sign on your hand, fix them as an emblem on your forehead, and write them on the doorposts of your house and on your gates.
>
> Deuteronomy 6:6-9

These words are a bold plea for people of all ages to remain involved in each other's lives.

I find the words of Psalm 78, a psalm of instruction, even more striking. These words probably come from the time of the divided monarchy and carry a strong warning to those present not to repeat the awful disobedience of previous generations. Listen for this idea in these words of Psalm 78:1-8:

> Give ear, O my people, to my teaching;
> Incline your ears to the words of my mouth.
> I will open my mouth in a parable;
> I will utter dark sayings from of old,
> things that we have heard and known,
> that out ancestors have told us.
> We will not hide them from their children;
> we will tell to the coming generation
> the glorious deeds of the Lord, and his might,
> and the wonders that he has done.
> He established a decree in Jacob,
> and appointed a law in Israel,
> which he commanded our ancestors to teach to their children,
> that the next generation might know them,
> the children yet unborn,

and rise up and tell them to their children,.
so they should set their hope in God,
and not forget the works of God,
but keep his commandments;
and that they should not be like their ancestors,
a stubborn and rebellious generation,
a generation whose heart was not steadfast,
whose spirit was not faithful to God.

We hear pain and fear in the words of this psalm. Asaph, the writer, is pleading for practices to be put in place that will minimize the possibility of future apostasy. If you read these words carefully, you will hear reference to at least four, if not five, generations. First Asaph speaks about "our ancestors" in verse 3, and then he speaks of "us" in the same verse. But he speaks of the "next generation" in verses 4 and 6. And again in verse 6 he refers to "the children yet unborn" and even goes on to the next generation: "they in turn would tell their children." Here is a clear picture of Asaph's concern that God's people remain faithful to God and that the generations must participate in the instruction and formation of each other for this to happen.

It seems that early New Testament–era believers lived with the assumption that, of course, the generations needed each other. This was an urgent concern among their ancestors in the Old Testament era, and we could expect it to carry over to new generations. So when Paul says to the Colossians, "Let the word of Christ dwell in you richly; teach and admonish one another in all wisdom" (Col. 3:16), we can assume that he pictures old and young in relationship with each other, for further in the chapter we find him specifically referring to wives and husbands, children and parents, and slaves and masters.

We get the best view of this connectedness in the pastoral epistles. When Paul exhorts Timothy concerning his ministry in Ephesus, he speaks of how to treat "an older man," "younger men," "older women," and "younger women" all in the same sentence (1 Tim. 5:1-2). We can infer that he must have seen the various age groups as part of the congregation. When Paul gives instruction and encouragement to pastor Titus on the life and behavior of the church, he raises the same subject. He encourages Titus to provide a setting where much instruction, admonition, encouragement, teaching, modeling, and training take place. And we also notice that he sees all age groups involved in this work. He mentions the "older men," "older women," "young women," "younger men," "slaves," and "masters" (see Titus 2:1-15). Each had a part in the formation of the others.

A Continuing Community

God wants his church on earth to be present through every age. So we speak about the perpetuation of the Christian church. This is not only God's desire, but it is also God's plan. On the one hand, the church will always continue because of his faithfulness in building it and preserving it, even through the most severe trials. And so Jesus could promise the disciples, "[O]n this rock I will build my church, and the gates of Hades will not prevail against it" (Matt. 16:18). In addition, the church will be perpetuated as it obediently follows the lead of the Holy Spirit in reaching and making disciples of others. Jesus said not only "Go therefore and make disciples of all nations" (Matt. 28:19), but also "[Y]ou will receive power when the Holy Spirit has come upon you; and you will be my witnesses in Jerusalem, in all Judea and Samaria, and to the ends of the earth" (Acts 1:8). So the church will continue here on earth because of the faithful work of Christ and the powerful work of the Spirit enabling people to make disciples of others.

But there is also a third consideration. Because the church will and must continue, each generation must shape the next generation so that each will know of God's mighty acts. The interplay of the generations in reminding each other of the truth of the gospel and the acts of God is an indispensable element of the continuation of the church. Even though missions and outreach are a key part of the church's ministry, we must acknowledge that more people have been brought into the Christian church by way of the Christian family and the instruction received there than through any other means.

When Ethan the Exrahite proclaims in Psalm 89, "I will sing of your steadfast love, O Lord, forever; with my mouth I will pro-

Karyn

Mark Stephenson

As a result of brain damage sustained as a child, Karyn lives with severe impairments. A few years ago Michelle, an employee at Karyn's group home, began taking her to a Friendship group. ("Friendship" helps churches share God's love with people who have cognitive impairments.) Although Michelle didn't attend church much, she thought the Bible lessons and music at Friendship were "kinda cool."

Later, Michelle and her roommate, Jenna, joined Karyn in going to her church. Michelle and Jenna grew in faith, attended membership classes, and joined the church.

One time Karyn's parents were sharing with Michelle their heartache over Karyn's severe impairments. They told Michelle that they hoped someday to know God's answer to their "why" questions.

Michelle confidently replied, "I can tell you why God allowed Karyn to be the way she is. God allowed Karyn to come into my life, so that my association with her would expose me to Christ, and as a result I would invite him into my life. Not a day goes by that my life is not affected by my relationship with Christ and with Karyn, and I'm going to tell this to everyone I know."

claim your faithfulness to all generations" (Ps. 89:1), he seems to have in view a people of God who continue through the generations because each age tells the next. So the continuation of the Christian church in society will depend on the faithfulness of the Christ who builds and protects the church, the Holy Spirit who empowers it to reach out, and the generations that form and teach each other.

Some Helpful Guidelines

If we look ahead 25 years, we see another generation in place. And if we ask whether that generation will know the Lord and walk in his ways, we should ask some questions about what we are doing now. Will our current efforts most likely be successful in helping the new generation come to know the Lord, be the church, and come to worship God? Should we perhaps worry about those who do not learn to worship with their families? Should we wonder if they will grow up never having built patterns of worshiping with adults? Should we be concerned that those who worship today in their own "age-appropriate" settings will not be able to make the transition into adult worship?

The march of the generations is proceeding. We adults were once children ourselves. And one day these children over whom we fuss and fret will be parents who fuss and fret over their own children. As the march of the generations goes on, the continuance of the Christian church depends on learning and developing healthy connections.

Becoming an intergenerational church is a complex task, one that will make the work of pastors and worship planners more difficult. Yet the work will be worth it. The values we are taught give us the highest motivation to continue our efforts to keep the generations being richly in relationship with each other.

Throughout this book, constructive ideas are offered to aid you in this work of building and maintaining an intergenerational congregation. After looking at all the biblical material in this chapter, let's spell out five guidelines that will be helpful.

1. *Consider all the chapters of life's journey to be equally valuable.* Often today we find that certain stages of life receive more concentrated attention than others. Out of concern for the healthy growth of children, a church will focus extra efforts on children's education. Because teens have so many struggles, youth ministry becomes a high priority. But when we view all the information from Scripture, we don't find any greater emphasis on one chapter of life than on another. God's work, Christ's attention, and the Holy Spirit's ministry do not favor one generation over another. Listening to the concerns and needs of parishioners convinces a pastor of the same thing. In my pastoral experience over 40 years I have been struck by the fact that Christians of all ages have struggles, questions, and growth issues. An 82-year-old parishioner once said to me, "In all your attention to the needs of youth, please don't forget that a lot of us older Christians still have a tough time

living the Christian life!" A 78-year-old man admitted to me that
he had expected that by this time in life his struggles with tempta-
tions and big questions would be pretty well resolved. "Not so,"
he said. If every chapter in life has its own unique needs and challenges, then all must remain in focus in our ministries.

2. *Avoid stereotypes.* Surely you've heard the stereotypes about
generational differences, and we all have a number of them float-
ing around in our heads.

"The children all prefer . . . "

"Twos are terrible."

"Youth all really like this better . . ."

"Seniors always . . ."

They are expressed so often that soon we accept them uncritically. We ought to be asking ourselves whether such statements are
true. Human preferences and behavior are just too complex to re-
duce them to sweeping statements like these. While some generalizations may be warranted, we need to be cautious about promoting sweeping stereotypes, especially if we are planning ministry
built on such stereotypes. Human beings are diverse, and diversity
appears both between the age groups and within each age group.

3. *Worship planning should be age-inclusive.* In chapter 10 we
will explore the issues associated with worship planning more carefully, but the matter ought to be raised here also. Those who carry
the responsibility for designing the worship services of a congregation have a much more complex task when the church is committed to intergenerational worship. Though we encouraged you to
avoid sweeping stereotypes, it must be admitted that different age
groups often do have different values and ways of communicating.
No one person can be expected to stay in touch with the desires
and needs of all generations, and so the group in charge of planning should be aware of and sensitive to the circumstances of each.
In the services they plan, the songs they select, and the prayers
they write and offer, the circumstances and needs of different age
groups must be represented. Those who are selected to read the
Scripture and to give leadership should represent all chapters of
life in the congregation.

4. *Encourage activities that prepare worshipers to be age-inclusive.* Many activities outside worship will influence how well

we can worship when we come together. By the time we enter the worship space, many influences have prepared us to relate healthily and comfortably with those of other age groups, or to feel uncomfortable and awkward. Parents who explain the main movements of worship to their children are preparing them well. Youth education classes that teach the basic principles of worship and explain the parts of the liturgy will promote healthy worship by youth. Service projects in which youth and adults serve side by side will make it easier for them to worship side by side. Fellowship opportunities like soup suppers and pancake breakfasts will provide healthy opportunities for being together. Teaming up youth and seniors as prayer partners reaps rich benefits in many congregations. Choirs that include several generations are good models for the entire congregation. Marva Dawn encourages that children's sermons be focused on teaching the parts of the liturgy to the children because it provides the essential preparation they need to be thoughtful worship participants.[1] Each congregation should aim to stretch its imagination to plan events and methods by which people are helped to live, work, serve, and talk together so they can worship together.

5. *Plan periodic worship events to be inclusive.* While most intergenerational worship will occur in the weekly pattern of a congregation's worship life, a congregation would do well to have special worship events from time to time that are more intentionally and obviously age-inclusive. These events will be able to speak more loudly and clearly about worshiping together.

Watch a video of your worship service and observe the ages of those in leadership. What conclusion would one draw about the nature of your congregation—that all worshipers are in their 50s, or that all ages belong here? For instance, imagine the beauty of an older man and his granddaughter side by side at the microphone reading Scripture. When we have distributed a worship resource bank survey[2] (appendix A) to ask for volunteers to lead worship, we have always encouraged volunteers of all ages. Often those who were younger and inexperienced needed some assistance and coaching, but such efforts were well worth it. Some congregations make sure that the visuals and art in their worship space or in the worship bulletin represent the efforts of both adults and children.

Prayer times in worship offer an opportunity to practice age-inclusiveness. When you listen to an audio or watch a video of your recent worship services, ask some questions about the intercessory prayers. Do they address the needs of all ages? Are the needs of children mentioned? Infants? Parents? Adolescents? Retirees? Age-inclusive prayers are a must in age-inclusive worship. If your congregation practices infant baptism, is attention focused on the children in the congregation? On parents? Grandparents? When adult baptisms take place, are other members of the family in other generations also visible? Are those who lead the liturgy always in the same age bracket, or is there inclusiveness?

The sermon is also an important time for integrating the ages in worship. Sermon material can be a helpful resource for explaining the needs of one generation to another. For instance, a message on young Daniel and his needs can provide a time to remind those who are no longer young of what adolescence is like, of the needs youth face, and of how much they need adults to encourage them. Similarly, a message about the death of Abraham can offer an opportunity to speak to adolescents and young parents about the concerns that seniors have as they reach their declining years. Let the generations experience dialogue with each other through the sermon. In appendix B, you will find the outline of a series of worship services, "The Chapters of Life," an effort to help the generations better understand and provide support for each other.

We should not shape our worship life for convenience or ease, or to satisfy popular preference; rather we should focus on biblical values that are timeless. The task we are given may be somewhat more difficult if we are faithful to these principles, but the result will be healthier and to the greater glory of God.

Discussion Questions

1. Review the five biblical values presented in this chapter.

   • Which value contains significant new insight for your congregation?

- Which value calls you to do more study and research to understand it better?
- Which value have you been neglecting that should receive closer attention?

2. Identify two or three stereotypes that your congregation has accepted uncritically. What can you do about that?

3. Evaluate the worship of your congregation during the past 12 months:

- Which services have been intentionally age-inclusive?
- Which elements of your worship service illustrate the greatest sensitivity to all ages?

4. If visitors were to worship at your congregation for five weeks, what conclusions do you think they would draw about your inclusion, or lack of inclusion, of all ages? What events or illustrations do you think they would cite to support their conclusions?

Howard Vanderwell is currently a resource development specialist for pastoral leadership at the Calvin Institute of Christian Worship and adjunct professor of worship at Calvin Theological Seminary. He previously served in the pastorate for 40 years. He is co-author of Designing Worship Together: Models and Strategies for Worship Planning.

CHAPTER 3

Worship and Faith Development

Robert J. Keeley

In the previous chapter it became clear that the formation of faith is one of the key values that the congregation must be concerned about. But how does faith develop? Through what stages does it go? And how will our knowledge of this process aid us in shaping the ministries of our congregations? Here Robert Keeley aids us by explaining how faith develops and the key role worship will have in that development.

Vital worship is a key element in the formation of our faith. Therefore, a congregation that aims to be spiritually formative must be keenly aware of the issues of faith development.

Faith is a gift from God, but the way faith shows itself in people of different ages and in different stages of life can vary greatly. The Christian community has a significant role to play in the development of that faith for all its members, so understanding the way faith develops is important to ministry. Our understanding of faith development as a construct comes primarily from the work of John Westerhoff and James Fowler,[1] both of whom are theologians and well-known authors on faith development. These two men have set out theories that help us understand the natural progression in faith that most of us pass through. Unlike cognitive development, which seems to reach its apex by early adulthood, faith development-at least according to Fowler's theory-continues on well into late adulthood.

Fowler points out that his theory is not just a theory of *Christian* faith development. He writes that faith is "generic, a universal

35

feature of human living, recognizably similar everywhere despite the remarkable variety of forms and contents of religious practice and belief."[2] Faith in something or someone is universal. All people, according to his theory, achieve their understanding of faith in the same pattern. There are many differences in the content of that faith, but the character of faith is similar for all people. We are interested in Christian faith development and how Fowler's theory will help us understand the people in our congregation.

It is important to understand the limitations of a theory like this. Developmental theories are usually fairly broad, and while we can sometimes get a pretty good idea of where people are in certain developmental areas, others are harder to pinpoint. It is rather easy, for example, to tell whether a child is able to use verbal language. Determining whether that child can understand abstract ideas is more difficult to assess. In the same way, it's difficult to measure faith development. While discussions of faith stages might cause us to think about specific people, we should resist the urge to pigeonhole individuals at a particular stage. As we think about this theory, it is good to remember that all developmental theories have three things in common:

- The order of passing through the stages is generally consistent from person to person. For example, in language, babies go from making only sounds to making words and then on to sentences. Few people begin with paragraph-length thoughts; their speech is usually much simpler.
- The amount of time one spends in any one stage varies. Some children speak much more clearly and much earlier in their lives than others, and there is quite a bit of variety in what is considered "normal" language development.
- The transition from one stage to another is gradual. The change from a state in which children cannot express themselves in words to one in which they can do so with ease takes a long time. The time between a child's first word and the point at which he or she has a relatively complete vocabulary usually involves years. Most normally developing infants begin babbling at about six months (a fact that seems to transcend cultures). By 18 months they have a

vocabulary of somewhere between five and 50 words, and by 24 months they have between 50 and 300 words. However, receptive language, the ability to comprehend, takes considerably longer.

Language is just an example of many types of development. In almost all areas it is difficult to pinpoint exactly where children are in their development. It is pretty clear, though, that there is a continuous process. While we can mark certain stages clearly (pre-speech or full speech with regard to language), in many cases it's tough to pin down what stage a person is in. Faith development stages can be thought of in the same way.

Faith Development

Fowler's theory of faith development is the most well known and most cited theory in the field. There are some criticisms of Fowler's theory—for example, that this is really only a theory of *Christian* faith development, or that we really shouldn't be talking about faith development at all; that it's a *relationship with God* that we need to be discussing.[3] It is also important to note that Fowler's theory is based heavily on the developmental theories of psychologists Jean Piaget, Erik Erikson, and Lawrence Kohlberg. Kohlberg's theory of moral development has been criticized for being too focused on Western males to be appropriately applied to a broader population. However, with an understanding that Fowler's theory is not the final word on faith development, we can still find his work helpful.

Pre-Stage

The faith development of babies is difficult to assess. Fowler calls this stage a "pre-stage" and refers to it as *Undifferentiated Faith*. This is not to suggest that nothing is happening with regard to faith but that we form our first pre-images of God in this stage. It is obvious that young children have a relationship with God, though. Psalm 139 tells us, "For it was you who formed my inward parts;

you knit me together in my mother's womb. I praise you, for I am fearfully and wonderfully made. Wonderful are your works; that I know very well." But we do not ask: "Does God know us?" The question is "Do we know God?" In a speech at Calvin College, noted theologian N. T. Wright told of being asked by a relative with a new baby how old children are before they first become aware of God. He responded, "About five minutes." He went on to talk about the connection between a newborn baby and its mother. If a baby can connect on a personal level with the mother at that young age, a connection with the God of the universe who made that child is not only possible; it is inevitable. Nonetheless, aside from pointing out the need for congregations to provide a safe and nurturing environment for children at church and to give support to tired and overworked parents, we will say little about children at this pre-stage in their development and move on to the first stage.

Stage 1

The first stage of faith, *Intuitive-projective Faith*, is found primarily in preschool children and is basically a reflection of their parents' faith. If we consider the cognitive development of children of this age, we understand that their reflection of their parent's faith is not the result of laziness or a lack of education. It is, rather, a completely appropriate way for children to begin their journey into the life of faith. According to the theory of cognitive development of Jean Piaget, children of this age are not able to think abstractly and are basically incapable of considering the world from anyone else's perspective. These children cannot think like a scientist, consider logical arguments, or think through complex ideas. Consequently, rather than having a faith that is carefully thought out, they have a faith that is based on impressions. These are impressions they get primarily from their parents but can get also from their faith community, their church. We can't expect preschool children to be able clearly and succinctly to discuss their faith. We can expect them to be able to tell us some of the stories of the Bible, to tell us that they love Jesus, and to begin to associate being in church with certain ideas. Rather than getting their information about God from lec-

Teaching Skills for Worship

Beth Ann Gaede

Our denomination had recently introduced a new worship book, and the congregation and I, their pastor, had a lot to learn about unfamiliar worship practices. I decided to try using the time designated for a children's sermon to teach about worship.

Each Sunday, I invited the children to the chancel, and I taught them something simple about worship: why the paraments were a different color that week, why we sometimes stood up and at other times sat down, why we had candles on the altar, what those odd symbols (an alpha and an omega) carved into the altar meant, what "Amen" means and why we say it with gusto, and so on. It was easy to keep the children engaged, because we usually had to move around the sanctuary—to look, touch, smell, or practice some liturgical action, or to make a simple liturgical response or sing a song.

Of course, the rest of the congregation learned alongside the children, and gradually the congregation grew in "liturgical literacy." We even sang Evening Prayer a cappella during midweek services in Advent and Lent. Over time, the congregation began using additional liturgies, which worshipers learned easily, in large part because they had developed a fundamental understanding of worship and the liturgy, as well as skills that transferred to a variety of worship settings.

tures or sermons, they will gather their impressions of God from what they see and hear and smell and touch.

We can minister to children at this stage in their development in a number of ways. Knowing that children will form impressions rather than dwell on specific topics or ideas should encourage us first of all to make our worship spaces beautiful. Children will build their first ideas about their faith from the impressions of what they see and hear in church. We should give them visual images that can stay with them and help them to begin to build accurate images of God. Much of the worship service, especially in churches that feature long sermons, will not connect to children of this age, but other parts certainly will. Much of the music, the rituals, and the readings are accessible to children. Repetition gives them an opportunity to build an understanding over time of certain parts of the service. Even much of what is said by the pastor or others is heard and remembered by children. On one Sunday when our pastor was away, a young woman from a neighboring church was our guest preacher. Before the children left for children's worship, she mentioned a bit of her personal story, including that she had recently had a miscarriage. In first-grade children's worship many children asked their teacher what a miscarriage was. These children *certainly* paid attention to what was going on in church.

The practice of removing young children from worship so that they can attend church school or their own worship service has generated much discussion. If children never see the inside of the sanctuary and they are never part of congregational worship, they never get the chance to see their parents, older siblings, and friends and relatives in worship. This image of mom and dad in church praising God is powerful, and we need to make sure children have an opportunity to experience this image. On the other hand, to honor their particular needs as members of the body of Christ, providing worship designed for their developmental level is also appropriate. Excusing children from part of worship so that they can see, hear, and touch things as they learn to praise God in a children's worship center honors the idea that they are image bearers of God with unique needs.

Stage 2

As our preschoolers get older, they move into the second stage of development, *Mythic-Literal Faith*. This stage begins around age 6 and normally lasts until about age 11 or 12. This is the stage of most elementary school children. During this period the Bible knowledge of children can greatly expand as they learn more of the stories of the Old and New Testaments. Although they are beginning to connect the stories, they really aren't yet ready for the mental leaps that would enable them to develop a sense of a larger, coherent story. These children are seeing the stories as disconnected individual stories that come from a book that they know is special. They are able to articulate their beliefs more clearly than they were before they began school, partly because of an increasing ability to articulate just about everything better. This change is an advancement in language ability as much as it is a step in understanding their faith. Still, these children, overall, believe pretty much what their parents have told them.

This belief is mitigated, however, by the information that children get from others. The circle of influence broadens beyond just parents in this stage; and others, including the faith community, have more of an impact. Some of this input from others can cause these children to have questions about the varied beliefs of their friends at school. It doesn't really occur to them that there are different ways of believing, so finding out that people they care about believe differently is a new experience for them. Even considering that others could have a faith different from theirs is a new concept for them. Being in a faith community is helpful as children of this age are looking around for confirmation that the faith they received from their parents is followed by others as well. Even without this confirmation, though, children of this age are still unlikely to question their faith or even wonder if there are other options. Their faith is what their family does, and that's the way it is for them. Their faith is tacit, unexamined.

We can be most helpful to children in this stage by continuing to recognize their developmental needs in worship. Fewer of these children will leave the congregational worship service to attend children's worship, so it is important that churches consider ways to keep these children engaged. This is also a stage at which these children should be learning more of the stories of the faith as found in the Bible. These children need to hear Bible stories in ways that allow them to take and keep these stories as their own. The people in the stories cannot just be flat characters who act nothing like any of the men and women that the children know. These stories need to be told to them in a way that lets the children explore the inner lives of the characters and, in doing so, to find their place in the story. These stories can't be just dry retellings of bland plots—they need to be shared by people with a passion for the truth that lies in the stories, and with experience and skill at sharing them in a way that makes them come alive.

Children also need to see that the Scriptures they hear in church school and at home have value for their parents and the other important adults in their life. They will gain much of that realization from worship. In some churches, much of the preaching is based on the Epistles, which will likely be less accessible than Gospel or Old Testament stories to these children. Including stories from the life of Jesus, from the book of Acts, or from the Old Testament will not only help these children to build a more solid understanding of a particular part of the Bible, but will also help them see that all of the parts of Christian truth connect. Clearly a diet of preaching that never addresses the Epistles is not appropriate, but neither is one that ignores or slights the stories of Scripture.

In his book *Faith Is a Verb*, Kenneth Stokes, a specialist on the dynamics of adult faith development, writes that this stage is also present in some adults. He suggests that adults who still find themselves experiencing their faith this way possess a faith that is "straightforward and literalistic."[4] They will often be most comfortable in a church that emphasizes a literal interpretation of Scripture along with a strong sense of both the authority of the Bible and of its religious tradition.

Stage 3

The third stage, according to Fowler, is *Synthetic-conventional Faith*. This stage will often begin about the time children enter middle school and last through much of high school, although some people remain in this stage throughout life. One of the primary psychosocial tasks of children at this age is to develop their own individual identities. The question "Who am I?" takes high priority. This stage corresponds with the emergence of what Piaget calls *formal operations*, the ability to think abstractly. These teens can see that they are unique and that they have an individual past and future. Their ability to think abstractly allows them to begin to put the stories of faith that they have heard over the years into a larger story—a story of the stories. They also begin to see the world from others' perspectives. This newfound ability has a large impact on the way middle-school children see the world and themselves.

Ironically, in this stage youth often begin to focus on the self more than ever. These young teens use this new ability to view things with others' eyes as a time to look at themselves more intently and to consider how they might appear to other people. If a middle-school student drops and scatters her books on the floor of the hallway in school, she assumes that everyone is looking at her and thinks less of her because of the mishap. It isn't just the trouble of having to gather up her things that bothers her; she really thinks that everyone who watched this happen is giving it as much thought as she is. That embarrassment can consume her, at least for a while. Realizing the dynamics at play here helps us understand the adolescent egocentrism that anyone who has lived with these young people knows all too well. Lynnae, an eighth-grader whose parents talked with her about this phenomenon, was able to recognize it when she read the first sentence of Rick Warren's *The Purpose Driven Life*. She closed the book and said, "This book is obviously not written for middle-schoolers." The first sentence is "It's not about you."

Even though she was able to recognize and joke about this aspect of her development, she was still convinced that some of her classmates went out and bought clothes just like those she had worn to school. She was able to joke about that part of being a young teen but was not always able to see when she was acting just like what she joked about. Part of the challenge of dealing with children of this age is that they are able to begin to grapple with abstract ideas and yet often have immature emotional responses to them.

At this age, people also want to begin to take charge of their own faith. A subtle but important shift happens between the previous stage and this one. In the previous stage children haven't really considered whether this faith is theirs; it just *is*. At this Synthetic-conventional stage the person *makes the choice* to accept this faith as his or her own. This is different from exploring other options and then deciding that the faith of your family is the best one. There is, for most adolescents, only one choice—the faith of their parents. That's the interesting thing about this stage: these young people really do make a choice, but there was actually only one item on the menu.

This is also a stage in which being part of a group is extremely important. Anyone who has had a son or daughter in middle school or who remembers what middle school was like knows the importance of being accepted by a group. This group both reflects and helps to form the identity of the individual. In some ways, the identity of the teen is determined by the people whom he or she chooses to be with. As teens grow and mature into the next stage, they will base their choice of friends on the identity of those friends to a greater extent than they do at this stage of development. But at this stage, just having friends is all-important. It is difficult to overemphasize the importance of peer relationships for young people of this age. This peer influence is also reflected in the way they grapple with matters of faith. Agreement and conformity are important. There is a strong desire to be like others—at least like *some* others—and so teens' faith will still mostly reflect the faith of those around them.

Teenagers' quest for identity will also cause them to emphasize the relational characteristics of God. They are naturally drawn to a view of God as One who knows them personally and who cares for them as individuals. While this emphasis can strike adults as incomplete or self-centered, it is an important aspect of coming to terms with their own identity and relationship with God. So this stage is curious in that one's faith is still, in many ways, unexamined; yet the people involved have made a conscious choice to follow this faith.

One of the important issues for all people in these stages is "Where is authority located?" For children in the early stages of faith development, authority is clearly located with their parents. One way to think of authority is to consider what children do if they don't feel well and need to stay home from school. Children are not allowed to answer this question for themselves; they have to persuade their parents that they are sick enough to stay home. When a child wakes up on a school day and complains about not feeling well, most parents do things like take their child's temperature or encourage the child to try to get ready for school and then see how he or she feels. Parents are gathering information to make that decision for their children while, at the same time, training them how to do it for themselves. As children get older, especially when they leave home, they increasingly make these decisions on their own until, eventually, even though they may ask for advice, the decision is theirs to make. Authority eventually lies inside them rather than outside.

For people who are in Fowler's Synthetic-conventional stage, whether they are teens or adults, the authority for their faith still lies primarily outside themselves. For young teens, the authority lies with their parents. Soon, however, it will shift so that it lies with a group—a group of friends perhaps, but often in the church itself. So for adults who remain in Stage 3, decisions about faith are based, in large part, on the answer to the question "What does the church say about this?" It is clear that some churches or other faith communities are set up to foster this viewpoint. Cults are one extreme example of a faith community that exerts control over its members. People in this stage will be most comfortable in churches that are clear about their expectations and about who makes decisions regarding personal faith issues.

Stage 4

The fourth stage, *Individuative-reflective Faith,* usually begins, if at all, during a time of personal change. It often involves moving away from home and beginning to take responsibility for more of one's own life, including one's faith life. One typical time for moving away from home comes when a student enters college. College campuses are full of young people who, for the first time, are grappling with their own faith apart from some parental authority. After a lifetime of not really questioning their faith, this stage finds people wondering whether their faith is really *their* faith. This is a time of doubt, of questions, and of uncertainty. It is a time when people ask whether the faith they have been given still "works."

While it might be easy to characterize this stage as a "college student" phase, research does not bear out this impression. In his study of adult faith development Kenneth Stokes found evidence of this stage throughout the adult life span.[5] People of many generations experience the kind of dissonance that comes with the real questions of faith that one begins to address in this stage of development. That does not mean that after this stage there are no questions, just as it does not mean that younger children have no questions about their faith. But at this stage, for the first time, people can hold their faith at arm's length and consider whether the faith they have been taught holds up to their questions. Some people simply opt out of religion when they come across clergy or others who won't work through the important questions that come. Stokes found that many people at this stage are told simply not to question their faith. He quotes a young woman who says that "it's tough being Stage 4 when you're surrounded by Stage 3 parents and preachers."

We are not talking about conversion or a change from one faith to another. Faith development stages are not about the *content* of faith as much as they are about the *character* of faith. A person who is in Stage 3, for example, and becomes dissatisfied with his or her faith community could easily leave that group and become involved in another faith community without experiencing any developmental growth. Some people jump from one group to another, relinquishing authority first to one group or charismatic leader and then to another. These jumps do not represent a movement from one stage to another. Cults, for example, depend on people engaging their belief systems at a Stage 2 or 3 level and don't hold up to the kind of scrutiny that comes with a Stage 4 level of development.

Understanding this stage also helps us understand why some people, a number of them in their 20s, might forsake a traditional church for one that is more progressive or experimental in worship style or for one that allows more individual expressions of faith. To people who are entering this individuative-reflective stage, a new and different way of expressing their faith resonates well with their desire to find a personal expression of faith rather than simply to continue in the tradition they grew up in, which they might come to see as shallow or not "real."

It would be a mistake to characterize certain styles of worship as being "less developed" or more attractive only at a certain stage of faith development, but it is also true that as people move into this stage they are looking for a faith community that speaks to their individual view of faith. People going through this transition might redefine how they worship and the faith community with which they associate. On the other hand, many people continue to find fulfillment in the faith community in which they grew up, particularly if this community is one that allows them to ask questions and to worship in ways that they see as "authentic." Relationships and the sense of fellowship that have been built over the years could trump the urge to "move on." Even though there is a strong

My Church Formed Me

Bethany Keeley

Fourteenth Street Church is where I learned what church community can be like, and where I developed gifts I continue to use today.

Fourteenth Street showed me a Christian community where people are valued. My peers and I formed friendships that began when we grew up together and developed through the years with good-natured teasing and deep love. This community, I soon realized, was a microcosm of what the church as a whole can be: authentic friends who support each other with the love of Christ.

At Fourteenth Street I also learned musical and leadership skills that I have continued to use. I developed as a musician from childhood by leading in church. That church family gave me the confidence (and sometimes forgiveness) to use my gifts and skills in corporate worship. When the community is more important than perfection, out-of-tune violin duets and pre-adolescent singing groups are treasured for their efforts to bring glory to God. These childish offerings became more mature gifts through experience and practice—gifts I now use in new communities to serve God and others.

Fourteenth Street taught me important ways God works in the church through people of all ages and talents, a lesson that continues to be valuable to me in all areas of life.

emphasis on the individual in this stage, the faith community is still important, especially if the community seems to represent a faith that is strong but not over-restrictive or dogmatic.

Stage 5

In Stage 5, *Conjunctive Faith*, the questions that first plague the Stage 4 believer have been put in perspective, and the tenets of faith that have stood the test of time make sense anew to the believer. In this stage, usually appearing no earlier than the 30s, all the threads that were present before come together. The believer experiences something like a second naivete. For many people this stage results in a realization that the faith that is practiced in well-established faith communities has much more depth and meaning than they gave it credit for during the time they were questioning and establishing their own faith. This is not a reversion to the earlier stage in which one's faith is unexamined. In sharp contrast, this is a time when faith is carefully examined but also when one's desire to stake out one's own faith territory with an individualistic conception of faith takes a backseat to a realization that the faith community has much to offer. In this stage, some of the earlier questions simply don't require answers. A person becomes more content with mystery, at least in some matters. In this stage a person is also ready for significant encounters with faith traditions other than his or her own.

People in this stage will want worship that mines the depths of their theology and also calls on the rich background of the faith community. In his chapter on this stage, Fowler writes that this position does not imply a lack of commitment or a "wishy-washy neutrality."[6] Rather, people at this stage of faith seem to have a radical openness to others' perspectives because they are so well grounded in their own faith. They see that the faith perspectives of others might well have something to add to their own mature understanding of faith. People in this stage of faith can truly appreciate symbols and rituals because they have grasped the depth of reality to which they refer. These people are ready for worship that is both progressive and ancient, individual and corporate, simple and complex.

Stage 6

Fowler goes on to write about a radical way of living out this faith in his discussion of Stage 6, which he calls *Universalizing Faith*. In this stage the ideals that one holds to in Stage 5 become actualized in the life of the believer. In Fowler's words, "Stage 6 becomes a disciplined, activist incarnation—a making real and tangible—of the imperatives of absolute love and justice of which Stage 5 has partial apprehensions."[7]

Threats to personal safety or to the safety of existing organizations do not deter the Stage 6 person from moving forward in his or her beliefs. Fowler characterizes this faith by pointing to people who have put their faith into action in unique and courageous ways, people like Mother Teresa or Gandhi. This stage is quite rare and is beyond the scope of this chapter and our work here.

Considerations for Ministry

The purpose of identifying the stages in faith development is not to enable those in leadership positions to encourage members to "move on" to the next developmental stage. The discussion of these stages is meant to be descriptive so that we can better understand the people in our churches. The developmental level of a person's faith has no impact on his or her salvation. Nonetheless, it is difficult to shake the notion that moving from one of Fowler's stages to the next is somehow an improvement. And in a sense it is. Faith development is, in some ways, like music appreciation. Consider two people, one who is highly trained in music and another who enjoys it but has no training. Both may be moved to tears by a beautiful symphony or a song. Yet the person with training appreciates the music more deeply, probably appreciates more types of music, and appreciates many more things about music than the amateur. Both of them can hear the same piece of music, and both can be moved by it; yet their experience is different. Both appreciate music; they just do it differently. Does the person who is knowledgeable about music have a "better" experience with music than the other person?

It could be argued that the amateur has a more "pure" experience with the music, much like the person looking at the stars in Walt Whitman's poem, "When I Heard the Learn'd Astronomer."[8]

No, Never Alone

J. George Aupperlee

> *Abide with me, fast falls the eventide;*
> *The darkness deepens; Lord, with me abide.*

Jane's verbal ability is severely limited by advanced Alzheimer's disease. Yet she softly sings these words with little hesitation. It is hard to say whether she understands what she is asking for in this prayer. However, it is clear that the Lord is keeping his promise to abide with Jane in these shadows that seem to envelop her life now.

Each week Jane joins other residents for worship designed especially for people with dementia. Touch, direct eye contact, and the use of individual names help contribute to a warm, personal, interactive worship experience. The chaplain presents a simple message of peace and comfort; the recreational therapist helps Jane participate in communion.

As Jane verbalizes every word of familiar hymns, the Lord's Prayer, and treasured Bible passages, it is evident that grace still flows through well-worn channels to the depths of her soul and keeps faith alive. The song she sings says, "Change and decay in all around I see." But when she receives a personal benediction, she gives a broad smile, indicating that amid the change and decay that bring anxiety and confusion, the One "who changes not" is abiding with her. The Light of the World penetrates the thick clouds of dementia and shines through the gloom.

At the end of each service Jane sings, "No, never alone, no, never alone. He promised never to leave me, never to leave me alone."

In Whitman's poem the careful mapping out of the stars robs them of their beauty. But Whitman does not suggest that all learning should stop. Neither does he suggest that the astronomer is incapable of looking up "in perfect silence at the stars." He merely warns us to keep our sense of wonder alive.

Jesus does something similar when he says, "Truly I tell you, whoever does not receive the kingdom of God as a little child will never enter it" (Luke 18:17).

This passage does not urge us to cultivate a shallow or childish faith, however. Rather, it reminds us that a relationship with Jesus, rather than a strict adherence to particular doctrinal standards, is at the core of our faith. In some ways, Jesus's admonition could be seen as advocating a higher stage of development rather than the sometimes simplistic faith of the earlier stages. It could be argued that the second naivete of Stage 5 involves a "re-wonderment" in our faith, an ability to recapture a sense of awe and mystery that is not as fully developed in earlier stages. Jesus's words have little to do with our developmental stage and much more to do with our willingness to put ourselves in his care.

Nonetheless, it is the role of the church to accept people at whichever stage they find themselves and to minister to them. A variety of faith stages will be represented in most congregations, and movement from one stage to another will be the result of maturation, experience, the role of the congregation, and the work of the Holy Spirit. We should not designate some churches for beginners and others for veterans. Living and serving together in an intergenerational setting make up an important component of the faith development of *all*. However, corporate worship is the defining event for most congregations. The way a congregation worships often sets the tone for all of the church's ministries. Therefore, we want to nurture the faith of all members.

In conclusion, here are some things to keep in mind as we aim to provide a worship life that will provide nurture for all:

- While children typically exhibit a level of faith development different from that of adults, they are also at a different cognitive level. Both of these considerations need to be taken into account. Worship leadership teams should have someone designated to ensure that every service has parts that are accessible to children, youth, and adults at all levels.

- While children's presence in worship is important, we will need to consider what sorts of things their faith is built on and what will nurture it best, and to make sure that those things are present in our worship—elements such as ritual, repetition, and familiarity.

- All worshipers need to be more than just spectators in worship. Examples of how to include them are discussed in other chapters in this book.

- Much of our faith is passed along through personal connections rather than through sermons. If possible, use worship to heighten those connections. Give children, youth, and adults opportunities to connect with those who lead worship and who worship with them.

- Adolescents, particularly, will feel more a part of the community if they are systematically included in worship through planning and participation in worship. These young people are adept at knowing when they're being given busy work. Make sure their inclusion is authentic.

- Young adults and others who are in the "searching faith" part of their faith journey will need sermons that explore difficult questions without simplistic answers. They will also benefit from post-sermon discussion groups and Bible studies in which they can explore these questions in more depth with mature members who are willing to engage the questions rather than just giving answers.

- Christians need worship that connects to their lives today while also allowing them to mine the riches of the church's past. Worship planners will be able to foster this balance through the use of the wisdom of other Christian traditions and cultures to enrich their worship.

- While we are accustomed to seeing children as being at a variety of developmental levels, we should remember that the adults in our congregations will also represent varied levels of faith development. One size will likely not fill all of the adults who sit in your pew on Sunday mornings any more than it will address the needs of all the children in your congregation.

Discussion Questions

1. Review the six stages of faith development that have been explained in this chapter. What insights does this theory provide for you in developing the ministry of your congregation? List from four to six insights for your congregation.

2. What does it mean for your congregation and its ministry that some adults may still show signs of Stage 2 (Mythic-literal Faith), as Stokes claims?

3. Evaluate the suggestions provided for the worship life of the congregation. Which are most helpful? What else would you add?

4. Identify several ways in which the worship life of your congregation has been sensitive to the stages of faith development in children and youth.

5. Identify several ways in which it seems your worship life has *not* been sensitive to these stages. What should be done about these?

6. Is the inclusion of children and youth in worship participating in your congregation authentic? Give examples of instances where it is authentic. Where does it seem to be less than authentic? What should you do?

Robert J. Keeley is an educator, professor of education at Calvin College, and chair of the Education Department. He has written extensively about ministry to children, including a recently published book, Helping Our Children Grow In Faith: Nurturing the Spiritual Development of Kids. *In addition to his teaching, Keeley is a musician and a worship planner at his congregation.*

CHAPTER 4

"Intergenerational" as a Way of Seeing

Gil Rendle

*A congregation that is successful in worshiping intergeneration-
ally has not merely found the right formula or the correct strategies; it has developed a whole new way of "seeing." The way we
see is shaped by many things, most of them related to the generation of which we are a part. Different generations often see
differently. Gil Rendle, on the basis of his study of congregations
and their behavior, helps us understand that recognizing the way
we see may hold the key for good conversations together.*

It was an odd step in a familiar liturgy and, frankly, I was stunned.
After a good deal of controversy the church was finally changing
the worship style of one of its several identical services, making it
less formal and more intentionally intergenerational. Part of the
design was to invite the youth of the church to distribute the elements of bread and wine during the Eucharist each Sunday that
the sacrament was celebrated at the early service. Even knowing
that this change was controversial did not prepare me for what I
saw. At the appropriate moment, the youth presented themselves
at the chancel rail to receive the elements for distribution. But before the bread and wine were handed over, the youth all presented
their hands, and the presiding minister walked from young person
to young person with a spray bottle of disinfectant. Each hand was
sprayed and wiped germ-free; the elements were then handed over,
and worship continued.

After some inquiry I discovered that an agreement to move
ahead with the intergenerational service had involved curious

steps of negotiation that, at one point, hung on some older members' concern about youth distributing the elements because of "where their hands may have been." The concerns were finally addressed by agreeing to disinfect the youth in order to include them in leadership. It was difficult to know whether plans for the service progressed because the concern of the few had been adequately addressed or because people had realized that the situation was sufficiently absurd to make further negotiations questionable. Yet here was proof that intergenerational worship could be planned in a way that made some feel like victors, some feel quietly demeaned, and others feel silenced, unwilling to name what was happening.

Generational Cohorts

One real dilemma of intergenerational worship is that it engages differing, and often competing, generational cohort values that live side by side in the congregation. People of different generations often like and enjoy being with one another. They may even see themselves as similar to one another, coming from the same families or living in the same community. Nonetheless, because of the cohort differences, discomfort below the surface commonly makes sharing worship, program planning, or decision making difficult across generations.

A generational cohort is that group of people who were born around the same time as one another and who learned the same life lessons because of their shared historical location in the culture that shaped their expectations. For example, members of the generation that experienced the Great Depression and the sacrifices of rationing during World War II learned about the need to protect assets. Knowing that whatever assets they had today might be gone by tomorrow taught lessons of thrift and the conservative use of money. Any unused assets were to be "saved for a rainy day." In contrast, members of the generation growing up in the 1970s and 1980s learned very different lessons about money. Growing up in a constantly expanding economy marked by inflation, they learned the new lessons to spend money today because there will be more

Web Logs and Worship

Young Kim

Our church community is associated with a large university campus. Most of our members are undergraduate and graduate students, with a smaller segment of working professionals, young parents, and their children. As a "younger" church, we are comfortable using computer technology. We use e-mail and navigate the Web every day. Many of us frequently update Web logs ("blogs") and maintain detailed profiles on social networking Web sites.

When we were challenged to explore the connection between worship and daily habits, we identified our use of the Internet as a habit we could potentially harness to reinforce the practices of Sunday worship. So we planned and implemented an eight-week integrated worship series that included weekly sermons, small-group Bible studies, artwork, original music, and a devotional blog that was updated daily with a new devotional reflection.

We used Xanga, a free Web log service, to host our devotional. We wanted as many of our church members to participate as possible, including our children, so each blog entry was a unique contribution from one of our members. Sunday school teachings went along with the series, and our children created artwork and wrote reflections expressing what they had learned. Their work was then scanned and posted as the devotion each Thursday. From the youngest child to the oldest adult, we all took ownership of our devotional blog.

We used technology to connect the generations in our church family.

tomorrow (the expanding economy), and to spend today because the money will be worth less tomorrow (inflation).

An intergenerational finance committee in a local congregation will no doubt involve people from different generational cohorts who like and enjoy one another. No doubt they will all agree that their task is to focus on the issue of faithful stewardship. Equally sure, as they work together some committee members will eagerly spend freely while others will think it's wise to save or protect dollars. These conflicting approaches to the use of money are grounded in very different life lessons, but the differences easily and quickly lead people to evaluate one another at a personal level. The reality, however, is that such personal evaluation is inappropriate. Asserting that some people are "cheap and too controlling" while others are "spendthrift and selfish" is not helpful. Rather, people are exhibiting differing but competing values learned during different life experiences. These competing values are appropriate to the historical moments in which these separate life lessons were learned.

The lessons each generation has learned, the values it has adopted, and its way of seeing serve as a lens or a filter through which the world is experienced and understood. Such generational filters lead to a natural conclusion, arrived at by each successive generation, that there is a "right way" to be in the culture. It is this assumption of a "right way" that leads to so much tension and misunderstanding between generations. Older generations quite naturally but mistakenly assume that the difference between them and younger generations (their children and grandchildren) is an issue of maturity. The assumption is that once the younger people "grow up," they will behave more appropriately—that is, they will dress better for worship, they will more readily sign on for committee and board responsibilities to help with the work load, they will sign a pledge card, they will. . . .

However, these are not issues of maturity but of differences. People with differing and competing values sit side by side in worship, as they do in all of congregational life. In one congregation a furor broke out when sneakers could be seen peeking from under the acolyte's gown as the altar candles were being lit. No matter that the cost of the sneakers would rival the cost of almost any other shoe in the sanctuary and that this was the "best" footwear the young boy owned. Because of their generational filter, several worshipers could only see a secular shoe intruding into sacred space. In this congregation one gentleman actually argued that the candles aren't really "lit" if the acolyte is wearing sneakers; therefore, worship should not begin. In other congregations the argument might not have reached such a pitch, but people would still express distaste and disagreement when others wearing sneakers, shorts, or T-shirts showed up in worship.

In another congregation everyone was excited by the prospect of the new children's choir. The church leaders had made plans to invite and include young families with children to participate in this ministry. A special Sunday was identified. The children were taught a special song. The parents were all especially invited, and they were present. Everyone smiled when the children stood to sing, and all went wonderfully—until the song ended. Then several people applauded. It was a natural response, but it set off extended conversations among the leaders for several months. They heard comments like these:

"This is not a performance."

"We don't come here to be entertained but to present our best selves before God in worship,"

"We came to participate. We don't want to be passive. This is an important place to us, and we present ourselves before God as we are, because by being here God can help us better discover who we are."

All of these rejoinders had a theology of worship embedded in them. In too many congregations intergenerational worship is simply a search for those compromises that will be most palatable or least offensive to the participants. Leaders too often go out of their way to head off conversations about differing expectations in worship, rather than helping members and participants to engage in and sustain essential conversations about how the congregation will now behave. Yet it is the conversations that engage the differing generational value systems that can bring some understanding and vitality to the congregation and offer a real future to the faith.

Bearing the Tradition

Because congregations are so *relational,* it is relatively easy to forget that they are also to be *purposeful.* In other words, congregations do exist for some purpose or purposes that go beyond bringing people together in community to support and appreciate one another. According to Dorothy Bass, director of Valparaiso University's Project on the Education and Formation of People in Faith, we can say that one of those purposes of a congregation is to be the "bearer of tradition."[1] It is the task of the congregation to bear the tradition of faith from one generation to another. Bearing the tradition does not mean passing it on intact, unchanged from earlier practice. Nor does it mean capitulating to the most recent fads and trends in music, movement, or the meaning of worship. Bearing the tradition means preparing to pass on the tradition to the new people *now coming* into the congregation as well as for those who have *not yet come* into the congregation. Bearing the tradition involves allowing new forms and practices that are fully embedded in ancient truth to reshape worship in a way that is sensitive to the eyes, ears, and hearts of those to whom the faith is to be given. This is a missionary task—holding the unchanging truth but shaping it to be understood in the present and changing culture.

Bass argues that congregations use two basic tools to shape the faith tradition and to bear it to the next generation. The tools are *argument* and *accommodation*. People in congregations argue about how to do things, and then as they accommodate one another in the argument, the practices of the tradition are shaped bit by bit to live in the changing world. In one congregation an older member pursued his case for limiting the selection of hymns to the old favorites. (He actually referred to a list of the 20 best hymns to sing—all of which were written in either England or Germany in earlier centuries.) The point not to be missed is that when others in the congregation proposed singing more contemporary hymns and songs from many cultures and continents, the ensuing conversation was an argument about much more than music. In fact, the people were deeply involved in a theological conversation about their understanding of their relationship with God.

Is salvation something that has been given exclusively to "us"? Those who answer yes to that question buy into an assumption held by earlier Eurocentric traditions. It prompted missionaries to convert people not only to the Christian faith but to a European or American lifestyle that would make these objects of mission more like the missionaries themselves and therefore more lovable to God. Or is God's love global—reaching across national, ethnic, and racial boundaries? Those who answer yes hold an underlying assumption that when we sing hymns from Mexico, China, or Africa, we are reminded that our own relationship to God is deepened and enriched by others different from us.

Far more than an argument about what music one person might like best, such conversations within congregations about worship are some of the most theological conversations our members and participants might be invited into. As the leaders and members of the congregation engage in the conversation about the appropriate hymnody for their church, they need help to sustain what can be a very valuable exchange, one in which the faith can be necessarily reshaped for a new day. Attempts at quick agreement or compromise that simply makes intergenerational worship palatable miss the opportunity of ministry. Congregations need the intergenerational conversations that lead to the practice of intergenerational worship as much as they need the intergenerational worship itself.

One of my favorite sayings is "There are a hundred ways to clean a kitchen, unless you are in your mother's kitchen." We each have generational defaults that tell us that a particular way of being, worshiping, relating to others, or volunteering is most appropriate. These default settings work well when we are alone or with our own cohort. However, we are each living with other generations of people in our congregations. Their way of doing things is not wrong, but their defaults are simply set differently from our own.

Preference and Purpose

To be intergenerational requires us to make the effort to see beyond our own cultural or generational lens. Being intergenerational is clearly a leadership issue. Being intergenerational is not limited to worship but includes programming, stewardship, mission outreach, even community formation itself. Being intergenerational is one of the most difficult challenges of congregational leadership in a fast-changing culture, because leaders must constantly be more focused on learning how to speak to the shifting culture than on speaking in familiar and safe language that is already embedded in the congregation.

A significant challenge in intergenerational congregations is to train and challenge leaders to look beyond the "preferential." The natural tendency of leaders in a voluntary institution such as a congregation is to satisfy the current constituency—to find the preferred way the current congregation likes to worship, to plan, or make decisions, and to embed those preferences as the approved

Mary

Robert Nordling

"This song will not work! It is Easter morning! It is inappropriate for our church; people will be offended and leave. This is wrong."

Mary was unhappy.

And maybe she had reason to be. I was messing with the style of our Easter morning worship service. Alongside the old standards—"Christ the Lord Is Risen Today," "Crown Him with Many Crowns," "Low in the Grave He Lay"—the choir was also going to sing a very up-tempo, gospel-style piece, complete with drums, bass, and guitars.

Half the choir thought it was a wonderful idea and loved the music. The other half—didn't.

"Well, Mary, Pastor and I have thought and prayed a lot about this, and we'd like to try including some newer music alongside the standards we sing. Our visitors recognize that style much more quickly than hymns. We'd like to give it a try, and I really need you to help us do it."

Mary was not thrilled. But for months, as we prepared that very challenging piece, she worked harder than anyone else to learn it. The offbeat rhythms, the extended harmonies, the vocal sound—all of this was brand-new to this faithful older member of the choir.

On Easter morning, Mary stood in the front row of the choir and sang that piece of music with all she had—and she *never* liked it. She did it because she understood that worship was not about her personal tastes, but was a community activity.

practices of the congregation. There are problems, however, when leaders simply follow the "preferred" ways too closely.

One problem is that when leaders simply endorse the preferred practice in the congregation, it becomes much more difficult for those leaders to hear and to respond to the new voices of people coming into the congregation. The preferred way is established as the norm and is not easily challenged. The necessary argument that will lead to faith-shaping accommodation will be missing because only one voice is allowed in the room. The deeper problem, however, is that when leaders assume it is their responsibility to satisfy the people who are already active members of the congregation, it becomes increasingly difficult to lead change and to learn new ways. One of the most difficult "kinds" of congregation to lead is the satisfied congregation because, quite naturally, it does not want to go anywhere different. Seeing intergenerationally means understanding that the task of leaders is far more than satisfying the members.

We need to understand that what satisfies most people is to remain in their preferred practice—their established *strategy* for doing anything from cleaning a kitchen to worshiping God. Strategies are ways, changeable ways, of reaching important goals. A principle in systems theory is that vital living systems must learn to be *steady in purpose* but *flexible in strategy.*[2] A species of bird must be steady in its purpose of finding food but flexible in its strategies for finding that food as the environment changes and, for example, former woodland or farmland is plowed under and a new development of homes replaces the former food sources. To be too rigid about practices appropriate to finding food in the woodland could be fatal when seeking food in the new housing development. Congregations too commonly mistake strategies for purpose and hold on to particular strategies as if the practice were itself holy rather than a way one might approach the Holy.

In a delightful conversation with the priest of an Anglican congregation in North America that was the daughter church of a parish located in England, I was told about a Christmas Eve tradition that discouraged people from coming to worship. The priest explained that the musical setting for the Christmas Eve liturgy was dismal, and few liked it. It was used year after year because it was the setting inherited from the famous mother church in England. The priest had tried unsuccessfully for nine years to change the liturgy for this important worship experience, but throughout those nine years, the church continued to send a steadily decreasing number of increasingly depressed people out to meet Christmas Day. Able to manage his frustration no longer, the priest called the choirmaster of the mother church to ask how that church managed with such a uncelebrative Christmas Eve liturgy. "Oh, that!" replied the choirmaster. "That setting was terrible. We stopped using that about 35 years ago."

Leaders must look at worship and other congregational practices from the perspective of purpose rather than preference. Rather than asking how most people *like* a particular practice, leaders must learn to explore how choosing a practice will most faithfully fulfill the purpose of the congregation. Daniel Schecter, co-director of the liturgy development project in the Reformed Jewish Movement, developed a procedure for self-study of congregational worship that helps congregations do just that.[3] Beginning with a worship team of eight to 12 people chosen to be intergenerationally representative of the congregation, the rabbi and the president of the congregation would instruct the team about the *purpose* of (not their current or preferred *way* of practicing) portions of the worship liturgy. Team members would then attend a number of worship services, keeping a "worship diary" in which they would record their feelings and reactions to portions of the liturgy. Their diary responses were copied, without their names, and circulated to other team members. The rabbi and president would then lead discussions about how worship in that particular congregation could be practiced in the most meaningful way.

Rather than settling into the default mode that most satisfied the strongest voices in the congregation, and rather than making arbitrary changes to worship that would, it was hoped, be palatable to most, this process was a clear effort to identify the timeless purposes of liturgy and then to engage people in a meaningful and instructive conversation about the most effective strategies to use in the congregation. Worship planners will help deepen the worship life of the congregation when they increase the congregation's awareness of the power and purpose of their worship. In addition, the community life of the congregation will likewise be deepened as generations engage one another in a healthy conversation to reshape the practice of the faith in an appropriate way.

The Bimodal Congregation

The argument in this chapter is that intergenerational leadership is a way of seeing—a way of seeing each other, a way of seeing the purpose of the church, a way of seeing the need to be flexible in our strategies for worship, leadership, and decision making. To be intergenerational, leaders need to be prepared to share the leadership table with people of different "cohort values" and to appreciate the differences that these others will bring. In a good number of congregations the challenge of developing an intergenerational way of seeing means getting the right people around a safe table for the conversations needed. The very makeup of congregations can make this conversation difficult to establish, however.

In a study of established congregations I worked with over a 14-year period as a consultant, a dominant profile emerged in which most congregations had a large number of people who had been members for 20 years or more.[4] These congregations also had a large number of people who had been members or active participants for 10 years or less and a much smaller number of people "in the middle" who had been members for 11 to 19 years. A graph of the tenure of membership in these congregations reflected what is statistically known as a bimodal distribution—an inverted, bell-shaped curve—which had large numbers of both long- and short-tenured people at the ends of the curve and a significant dip with few people in the middle.

What was most instructive to my work as a consultant was that the two dominant subgroups at the ends of the curve—the long-tenured people and the short-tenured people—reflected very different and competing generational values and behaviors. Here is where the deepest differences between generational cohorts live in congregations. In worship, for example, long-tenured members tend to focus on formal, traditional practices of worship that favor uniformity, music out of a European tradition, and clergy-centered leadership. People attending are *recipients* of worship. Short-tenured members and "participants" (a growing percentage of people now active in congregations choose not to join as members but are nonetheless committed participants) tend to focus on less formal and less traditional practices of worship that favor spontaneity, contemporary music, songs from a diversity of world regions and cultures, and shared leadership. People attending are active *participants* in the liturgy, and ancient practices are updated and renewed for a new day.

When working with congregations, I frequently conduct a tenure study, measuring the percentage of the congregation that has been there 10 years or less, 11 to 19 years, and 20 years or more. These three measures allow me to see the inverted bell curve, and they offer some sense of the strength of the cohort voices in the congregation. I then commonly do a second tenure study of only the key leadership people and groups such as the governing board. Of those on the board, what percentage have been there 10 years or less, 11 to 19 years, and 20 years or more? It is important that the leadership tenure curve closely reflect the membership/participant tenure curve. All too often I work with congregations whose membership/participant tenure curve has its strongest tail (the largest percentage) in the short-tenured group—the people there 10 years or less—but the leadership tenure curve has its strongest tail in the long-tenured group, people there 20 years or more.

Frequently this common situation in long-established congregations results in a stagnancy of growth and development in the ministry of the church. Long-tenured leaders end up planning worship and programs that are intended for others, for people whom they don't quite understand and who therefore will not want to participate—programs that the long-tenured leaders themselves hope *they* will not have to attend. Rather than actively engaging the practice of the faith, the energy in these congregations tends to become increasingly depleted because the right (that is, "different") voices are not in the room and at the leadership table.

Using Bass's construct of bearing the tradition, leaders in intergenerational congregations engage in arguments and accommodations. Care has to be given, of course, to be sure that people feel safe when they explore their differences. In his seminal work on leadership, Ron Heifetz, former director of the Leadership Project at the Kennedy School of Government at Harvard University, suggests that leaders address the need for safety by providing a "holding space" where people can engage differences safely and with energy.[5] In fact, it can be fun. People naturally understand these differences, and they confront them every day in their work, in their families, and in their friendships. In the last congregation I served as pastor, one of our members was the president of a local utility company, and he loved to tell the story of the day a new

A Norm

Jimmy Setiawan

In my denomination in Indonesia, "intergenerational worship" is still a foreign *concept,* let alone as a *practice.* Since the church's founding 56 years ago, it has been a norm that our worship services generally are designed for those of at least college age. Of course, this norm is not applied consistently, but three things prove that it is very much alive.

First, the worship planning team, including the pastors, chooses the themes for weekly worship with an eye to a congregation that is young adult and above. Secondly, we have a separate worship service for adolescents. If a teenager visits our worship service for the first time, he or she is encouraged to join the youth service instead. Third, there are three slots of Sunday school times, parallel to our three worship services, so that the worshipers can send their children to the Sunday school while attending worship. They feel that to bring the children into the worship service would be improper because the children could be a distraction.

As I think about the concept of intergenerational worship, I am allured by the beauty of the concept. However, bringing the concept to reality will be hard work, requiring a lot of wisdom and patience. Otherwise, it could be just another divisive matter in the church.

secretary started work in his office. Midmorning of that first day, he asked his new secretary, a woman considerably younger than he, to get him a cup of coffee. "Yes, of course," she replied. "But tell me," she continued, "when did you break your leg?" It was clear that she did not expect to fetch him coffee and that he had stepped into a deep generational difference regarding expectations of the secretary's role. The executive had a choice—to accept the response of his new secretary with the humor in which it was offered, or to make it into a battleground over power. He and his secretary went on to talk about their expectations of her role. And he was free later to tell the story of that first day to his friends with good humor and great laughter.

A Way of Seeing

Intergenerational as a way of seeing is an act of Christian hospitality—rich Christian hospitality. Too many congregations limit their practice of hospitality to politeness. This form of hospitality is like fixing your home up just the way you like it and then inviting friends in to share it with you. All is well and good as long as the friends play by the rules. But as soon as a friend picks up the remote and changes the channel on the TV while you are watching it, the politeness is over and ownership reasserts itself.

I was confronted by the difference between politeness and hospitality in my last congregation soon after we began sharing our facilities with a new church in the Latino community surrounding us. We hired a pastor from Puerto Rico and provided worship, program, and office space. However, we also unwittingly provided many expectations about how that space was to be used. Finally, my Puerto Rican colleague had to come to me and, speaking for his congregation, say, "It is wonderful to be invited into our brother's house. However, it is not easy always being reminded that it belongs to our brother."

Intergenerational worship, programming, stewardship, decision making, and faith formation require so much more than politely allowing others to do it their way "in our church." It is a way of seeing and being with each other that goes deeply beyond politeness to true hospitality, where we see God in one another and shape a new community because of what we see.

Questions for Reflection and Discussion

1. What new changes or practices have been introduced into the worship or programs of our congregation in the past few years because of the presence of new generations? How have these changes enriched our lives and deepened our faith?

2. What examples can we identify in our congregation of generational cohort differences popping up and creating disturbances or disruptions?

3. What strategies (practices and ways of doing things) have become so sacred in our congregation that we would have to struggle to change them even if they no longer accomplished their purpose?

4. When natural and normal differences between generations pop up in our congregation, is it our tendency to laugh, appreciate them, and talk about our different expectations, or to become quiet, move toward opposing subgroups, and struggle over power?

5. Does the makeup of our leadership group closely reflect the makeup of our full congregation of members and participants?

Gil Rendle is senior consultant at the Leadership Institute of the Texas Methodist Foundation, Austin, Texas, and independent consultant to congregational systems. Previously he was vice-president for program at the Alban Institute, where he served as senior consultant and a director of education and consulting. For nearly 20 years he has worked as a consultant with local congregations and judicatories. He is an ordained United Methodist clergyperson with 15 years in parish ministry.

CHAPTER 5

Fostering an Intergenerational Culture

Darwin Glassford

Intergenerational worship should not be seen as a product of our planning sessions. It's not merely a matter of doing certain things or implementing certain practices. Healthy intergenerational worship will not take place apart from an entire ethos or culture of intergenerational relationships. This chapter calls us to see the bigger picture of all relationships. Glassford helpfully calls us to aim for an entire culture of intergenerational relationships. Note how he uses his current denomination, the Christian Reformed Church, as a case study of the culture to be fostered.

Intergenerational worship is a countercultural activity. In a culture that segregates and isolates children, preteens, and teens, and then appeals to them separately, the church is a truly countercultural community when it invites all generations to participate actively in worship. However, intergenerational worship is an essential element for the church that is going to retain a character and ministry consistent with the Bible.

Israel's worship in the Old Testament was intergenerational. Children camped with their parents during the Feast of Tents (Lev. 23:33-43); children inquisitively questioned their parents about the significance of Passover (Exod. 12:1-28; Deut. 16:1-8); children as a part of the worshiping community experienced the sights, sounds, and smells of the sacrificial rituals (Lev. 16; Deut. 15, 19). Israel's worship was intergenerational, and so should the church's be.

Jesus welcomed the children. Paul described the church as the body of Christ (1 Cor. 12:12-26). Peter highlighted the continuity between Israel as the people of God and the church (1 Pet. 2:9-10). We profess these truths but do not generally integrate them into our worship practices, and therein lies our culture problem. Children, preteens, and sometimes teenagers are often seen as bothersome. They are seen as a distraction during worship; they ruin the experience. Worship, however, is not an adult activity. It is an activity of the faith community.

Three questions need to be explored to foster a culture that promotes intergenerational worship:

1. What contributed to the decline of keeping the generations together?
2. How fluid and changeable is the body of Christ as a metaphor?
3. How then shall we equip the body of Christ for intergenerational worship?

In the process, we will discover that intergenerational worship must be grounded in Scripture and will require the development of an ethos or culture of deep relationships in which we seek the good of others and respect one another regardless of age, sex, or any developmental considerations.

Before engaging the first question, the reader should know that my primary interest is in the educational dimensions of worship. I am absorbed by what is learned in and through the act of worship. Educationally speaking, we sometimes teach *intentionally* (explicit curriculum); we teach other things *by the methodology employed* (hidden curriculum); and we teach *by what we omit* (null curriculum). For example, imagine a situation like this—a middle-school boy sitting in the balcony drops the offering plate loaded with coins. Certainly he receives a scolding from his father, as well as a stealthy glare from the usher. I do not think, however, that he learns to be more attentive. He learns only that in church one cannot have accidents. He learns that church is not a safe place. As we address this topic, we must be attentive to what we hope to teach and to what we may be teaching unintentionally. And we should also remember that though we may desire to teach one thing, what is learned may be something quite different.

What Led to the Decline of Intergenerational Worship?

Attempting to make worship intergenerational involves a commitment to all people of all ages that they will share the same level of significance and worth in worship. Worship of this sort was generally practiced, at least on the surface, throughout much of the church's history. While all ages were in the same pew, it would have to be admitted that most worship was planned with adults in mind. So being intergenerational may have been something of a myth. It is difficult to discern what led to the development of parallel worship services: one for young children, in some cases a separate service for teenagers, and another service for the rest of the congregation—"big people's church." In the Christian Reformed Church, the tradition with which I am most familiar, the movement in this direction is typical of many. Two historical markers illustrate the decline of intergenerational worship.

A Shift in the 1960s and 1970s

Though trends generally develop slowly and sometimes almost imperceptibly, it seems that the shift to the practice of having young children leave worship before the sermon for an alternative, "age-appropriate" worship service developed during the early or mid-1960s. It gradually became apparent that many congregations across the nation were increasingly adopting this innovation. In 1967 Hugh Koops, then assistant professor of Christian education at Western Theological Seminary in Holland, Michigan, observed the church scene and wrote about "the simple fact that a growing number of congregations are moving in this direction."[1] Two congregations serve as examples of what many were beginning to do—one in Seattle, Washington, and the other in Grand Rapids, Michigan. A description of this practice first surfaced in *The Banner*, the official publication of the Christian Reformed Church, on

November 12, 1976 (the two churches cited were affiliated with this denomination).

In a letter to the editor in *The Banner,* written by "Grandma," we find:

> Some time ago our church started a "Children's Church" so called, at the urging of some members, and now the children age 3–6 regularly leave the church before the sermon and go over to the Christian school building where they, with some volunteer adults, have their own service.
>
>   . . . I have concluded that we are robbing those children who leave of something unique and inestimably precious.

She then describes the practices she and her husband had with their four children in worship. They sat with them and saw to it that they "got a good dose of church atmosphere"—and by that she meant "organ music, stained glass, the reverent hush; and more importantly, witnessing and hearing some four to five hundred real live adult Christians singing psalms and hymns, praying together, opening Bibles, and listening attentively." Then she observes:

> In trying to do more for the child we rob him of an example so remarkable and rare that it is impossible to overestimate its benefits; namely living Christians worshiping their Lord.
>
>   And rob them for what purpose? I'm afraid it's to almost no purpose because every child must still be taught sooner or later to sit still in church, and sooner is often easier than later. It doesn't relieve the busy parents very much at all, just gives them tougher problems later.[2]

Three observations are in order: (1) "Grandma" does not specifically address the reasons why these members requested the alternative service; (2) the alternative service is being provided by volunteers; and (3) she is concerned with children sitting still.

In a response to Grandma's letter in a later issue, another reader responds: "It might surprise you to know that these little ones sing Christian hymns, dedicate their offerings to God, say prayers,

Welcoming Children

Taka Ashida

In my congregation in Tokyo, Japan, three boys—seven, five, and three years old— needed to be welcomed in worship. Their father brought them each week by himself. Their mother, not yet a Christian, did not attend.

But usually, when they came with their father, the boys had not been allowed to join the worship service in the sanctuary because they were noisy. They and their father remained in the entrance hall during the worship service, quite separate from the rest of the congregation.

Soon after I became the pastor at the church, I asked the father to bring the boys into the sanctuary during the worship service. They needed us; we needed them. He was happy to hear that from me.

Some members accepted the boys, even though they were not always so quiet. Some complained because they like to worship God in a calm and quiet environment. I thought it was necessary to teach the congregation how important intergenerational worship is, so that during Sunday morning services we would enjoy a foretaste of the ultimate worship service in heaven. Even a little noise should not stand in the way. It is difficult for some to understand this significant truth perfectly, but our welcome of the children showed the hospitality they needed.

listen to Bible lessons, and learn the elements of adult worship, following a liturgy quite like yours and mine." She goes on to state that "Children's Church is not meant to relieve young parents of their responsibility, but rather as an aid toward developing a positive feeling of community and worship among those beloved ones of His flock."[3]

This response is important because it introduces two categories of worship—adult worship and children's worship. The letter also indicates that a well-developed alternative worship program for children is being conducted at the reader's church.

The question of why these churches created alternative worship services for young children remains unanswered. This is not an isolated exchange. Hugh Koops in 1967 observed not only that the practice of providing alternative services for children was increasing, but also that he believed that this increase could be attributed to the reality that worship was increasingly viewed as a teaching service for adults. He asserted that the sermon had become the major instrument for adult education rather than a proclamation of what God has done in Jesus Christ; the sanctuary had become a classroom for adults rather than worship for all generations, and consequently children found themselves "in the wrong classroom on Sunday morning."[4] This shifting view of worship, combined with new insights from developmental psychology that emphasized teaching for learning, rather than preaching for response, created a fertile environment for fostering alternative worship services for children.[5]

Discussions in the 1980s

Discussions about intergenerational worship continued to take place. A pivotal part of the discussions concerned the legitimacy, if any, of an alternative service for children. In 1988 the publication arm of the Christian Reformed Church reported to its annual synod (or general assembly) that it had endorsed a children's worship curriculum that used "the Berryman/Stewart approach"[6] rather than the development of alternative services for children.

The Berryman and Stewart curriculum was based on the pioneering work of Sofia Cavalletti.[7] A religious educator of young children and author on the subject, Cavaletti wrote about her work with children in *The Religious Potential of the Child*. The curriculum was rooted in developmental theory and was experiential in nature. It sought to teach young children about worship in a developmentally appropriate manner. The curriculum stressed the use of the imagination and godly play in assisting young children to appreciate the mystery and wonder of worship. It provided a unique resource for churches that desired to support or create an alternative worship service for children. The Children and Worship curriculum, the shift toward understanding worship as a teaching service for adults, and the desire to maximize the learning of children and adults created a unique context that contributed to the decline of holding all ages together in public worship.

We can observe two things from these discussions that will influence our understanding of intergenerational worship and assist in our evaluations:

1. *Language is important.* A distinction between adult worship and children's worship was introduced. Both were called worship. Worship is an activity of the body of Christ—the community of faith. When the church gathers for worship, the body of Christ gathers. When children are separated out, and the activity provided for them is called an alternative worship service, the nature of the discussion about worship changes. Instead of a community event, it is now a developmental matter that attempts to be age-appropriate.

2. *The purpose of worship must be clear.* Is worship a corporate activity of the body of Christ or a teaching service for adults? Educationally, if worship is seen as a corporate activity, then the socializing role of worship will be emphasized. If worship is understood as a teaching service for adults, then the need for a developmentally appropriate alternative service for children will be advanced. For this reason, the two groups advocating these opposing points of view often talk past each other and find it difficult to have a productive discussion.

The introduction of the idea of alternative worship services for children illustrates the many challenges of congregational worship that still need to be addressed. The presence of alternative services reminds us that genuinely intergenerational worship is undermined when sermon illustrations engage only one group in the congregation and overlook others who are present; when young people and their culture are marginalized; or when the experiences of children or of any group are neglected. For worship to be genuinely intergenerational, it must be pursued; it does not just happen.

The Dynamic Nature of the Body of Christ Metaphor

But there is also another matter we must consider. When we aim to foster worship that includes all the generations of a congregation, we must carefully consider the larger context in which it happens. Worship and the role of its various elements are best understood in the light of the metaphor the Bible uses of the church as the body of Christ. The individual preferences we may hold, the experiences and history that have shaped us, and the cultural context in which we live all must be considered; but the biggest consideration of all is that the church is the body of Christ.

This body of Christ metaphor employed by Paul is dynamic, filled with significance and movement. Its central premise is "[Y]ou are the body of Christ, and individually members of it" (1 Cor. 12:27). This metaphor serves to fashion "a new vision, the birth of a new understanding"[8] of the church. Seeing the congre-

---

Advent Wreath

Karen DeMol

During Advent, our congregation has an Advent wreath as part of its worship. Each Sunday, Scripture passages are read, prayer is offered, and another candle is lit. This year the committee decided that on each Advent Sunday a parent-child pair should lead us—a father and a daughter, a mother and a son. In addition to the generational difference in these pairs, there is a height difference—tall mothers, even taller fathers, much shorter young sons and daughters.

To enable the young ones to reach the lectern reading surface and the microphone easily, the committee placed a bright blue Fisher Price stepstool behind the lectern. Functionally, this worked fine. But the best part was the sweet snapshot created in my memory of seeing the heads of the parents and children on the same level as they took turns reading the Scripture selections for the day to the congregation.

gation in this way invites us to re-evaluate and reform our practices. Paul employs this metaphor to assist the Corinthian church in understanding itself, which is necessary if the Corinthians are to constructively address the issues they face in community life and worship. According to the metaphor, every person is essential. When one person is absent, neglected, or marginalized, the body suffers, and worship ceases to be inclusive. Worship that pays attention to all ages aims to capture and implement the reality of this metaphor of the church as the body of Christ.

Christ is the head of the body, the church. Paul, in his letter to the church at Ephesus, emphasized this conviction when he wrote, "[S]peaking the truth in love, we must grow up in every way into him who is the head, into Christ, from whom the whole body, joined and knit together by every ligament with which it is equipped, as each part is working properly, promotes the body's growth in building itself up in love" (Ephes. 4:15-16). It is Christ's church. It is not our church. Fostering a climate that is conducive to intergenerational worship means that both the leadership and the congregation must endorse this truth that they are the body of Christ.

Fostering such a climate in Christ's church includes valuing, nurturing, and employing the gifts of every person (Rom. 12:4-6). It celebrates the children who participate. It rejoices with the young person who expresses his faith through an instrumental guitar solo. It waits patiently if an elder member of the congregation needs more time to light the Advent candle. It listens attentively as a member publicly reads Scripture. It rejoices when a child first participates in communion. It weeps when someone's gift is marginalized or neglected. It gasps when the child stumbles during the liturgical dance, because her "embarrassment" is felt by all. It experiences the young person's "frustration" when a note is missed. It feels awkwardness when the person reading Scripture stumbles over an unfamiliar name. Genuine intergenerational worship involves the body of Christ rejoicing and suffering together because of the members' love for and commitment to each other.

The body of Christ metaphor summons the members of Christ's body to a lifestyle of selflessness that will promote spiritual maturity. Paul illustrates this in 1 Corinthians 8 when he addresses the thorny issue of eating meat sacrificed to idols. The Corinthian church, in dealing with this issue, was struggling to discern what it meant to follow Christ faithfully in its particular context. This passage illustrates the challenges of dealing with thorny issues and provides three helpful clues to understanding the relationship between a selfless lifestyle and spiritual maturity.

Clue 1: Paul addresses a difficult question in a clear, specific, and pastoral manner when he explores whether it is permissible to eat meat sacrificed to idols. If we desire to foster intergenerational worship, it is essential that we ask questions with those qualities. Our questions must not be vague and hurtful; for example, "Why aren't teenagers more responsive in worship?" The sentiment and question clearly could be rephrased in a positive manner. For example: "What actions in the worship service clearly address the unique needs of our teenagers?" or "How can we help our children pray better in public worship?"

Clue 2: Paul provides an alternative perspective on the issue. He reminds the church that Christ is the Lord of all and that "food will not bring us close to God" (1 Cor. 8:8). The significant differences in Corinth were the result of an inadequate understanding of Christ. Fostering intergenerational worship requires looking at issues from a different foundational vantage point. For example, rather than arguing for a traditional or a contemporary style of worship, we ought to strive to discern the biblical truths about worship. Is it about style and form? Or is it ultimately about a community of diverse people engaging with God? If we pursue biblical truths, we will quickly see how the line between personal preferences and scriptural teaching becomes clearer, or at times even disappears. When the Bible talks to us about meeting God in prayer, we are lifted to thinking about bigger things than personal preferences. Discussions of personal preferences outside their scriptural underpinnings are often personally and corporately disconcerting. Could we ask, for example, "What eternal truths are we projecting when we provide an alternative worship service for children or teenagers?" or "What does the range of musical styles used in worship teach us about God?" or "What impression of the nature of God comes through when we are required to worship separately?"

Clue 3: Paul addresses the issue with respect for all. He respects the consciences of those who have not yet sorted out this issue. He calls on those who feel that they are free to eat meat sacrificed to idols to respect the scruples of those who do not believe they ought to do so. He tries to avoid slipping into the "weaker Christian syndrome," in which a list of everything that offends any member of a congregation is implicitly compiled and prohibited. This approach does not foster a genuine intergenerational culture, nor does it promote spiritual growth within the body of Christ. Yet unfortunately, this is how we often function.

Paul offers another alternative. The "weaker" Christians are respected to keep them from sinning as well as to provide an opportunity to instruct them in the faith. To instruct, one must show respect. The "weaker" Christian is respected—meaning that those who are more mature in the faith may have to sacrifice their freedom for the sake of this brother or sister in the faith. Paul does not want the "weaker" Christian to remain weak. He or she must be instructed and taught to distinguish between scriptural warrants and personal preferences. The goal is spiritual maturity. If someone is offended by drums in worship, we respect that response while at the same time assisting the member to understand that all music has a beat and that a variety of instruments are employed throughout the Scriptures in worship. Our preferences are just that; we must be willing to sacrifice our preferences for the spiritual nurture and instruction of others. An intergenerational community ought to be characterized by a sacrificial attitude that desires to foster spiritual maturity.

Fostering an intergenerational climate is challenging because each person of the community must distinguish between personal preferences and scriptural warrant. We must value and respect the other members of the body of Christ; we must be willing to learn from each other; and we must seek to nurture the faith of others. We must confess Christ as the head of the church and seek to live in light of that reality.

Learning Together

Norma de Waal Malefyt

When I was a college student I had opportunity to accompany an adult choir at a neighboring church. This was a unique choir—40-plus strong, with members that included high-school students through those long past retirement.

We learned well together. The young could grasp rhythms that made the older members shake their heads in astonishment. The old had the ability to read music with a skill that made us kids envious. Together we encouraged each other in ways that made our learning efficient and fun.

But there was more than singing to this group—we really "fellowshipped" together. Following every Sunday-afternoon rehearsal we gathered in the church basement for a supper of sandwiches and the best bars and cookies any college student ever had.

And we prayed for one another. When illness or sorrow entered the lives of the people in choir, we prayed in ways that seemed more personal and pressing because we all knew each other. I made friends for life in that group, and I treasure the intergenerational relationships that were fostered there.

Years later, when I directed an adult choir, I sent letters of invitation to each high-school and college-age member of the congregation, communicating that very positive experience I had been privileged to have.

And some of them came and experienced anew what was so real and valuable to me.

How Then Shall We Equip the Body of Christ?

Fostering a climate in which intergenerational relationships thrive is a challenging task. Intergenerational worship is not only about how members of a congregation relate to each other in their worship, but also about the ethos surrounding their worship. Biblically authentic intergenerational worship is more than a program; it is a way of life. Fostering a new way of life is challenging because both the individuals and the community of faith must distinguish personal preferences from biblical standards. There must be a willingness to put aside one's preferences for the sake of others. There must be a willingness to wrestle with deeply held preferences and their biblical basis. Toward this end I will suggest six questions a church staff, committee, or community should consider to nurture an ethos that promotes an intergenerational culture.

1. *What do the Scriptures call the church to be?* What should be the distinguishing characteristics of a community of faith? We should not think in terms of programs, but in terms of character traits and values. For example, Paul offers a vision for the church when he summons the Ephesians to "the unity of the faith and of the knowledge of the Son of God, to maturity, to the measure of the full stature of Christ" (Ephes. 4:13, 16). What does Paul mean by "unity in the faith," "knowledge," and "maturity"? How are these characteristics related? The discussion should engage the imagination; it should invite participants to see things differently (see also chapter 2).

2. *How well does our congregation understand intergenerational worship?* Reflect carefully on the life of the congregation. Do members understand why we have a children's sermon? Do they insist on quality in the children's sermon, or are they willing to tolerate a poor one? Do they apply the same standard to adult participation as they do for that of children and youth? Discern why certain practices in the life of your congregation were adopted. Study their history. What has been helpful? What has not been helpful?

3. *What ought to characterize a genuine intergenerational worship service?* You may try to begin with a blank slate so that you are not bound by a traditional pattern, but it is somewhat difficult to avoid any kind of template at all. Do not try to fix or improve on what you are currently doing. Design a new order of worship for a service that will be hospitable to all ages. Describe how the layout of the worship space and furniture contributes to or undermines such worship. Discuss what the selection of musical styles communicates to the various populations that attend the church. Be sure to consider Scripture and scriptural images as you

wrestle with how various age groups would respond to the various components of the worship service.

4. *What are the implications of the body of Christ metaphor for the local church?* Study it and reflect on it. Use it as a lens through which to question your preferences, understandings, and practices. Wrestle with why you may tend to value some gifts and their expression more than others. Ask whether some age groups are catered to in worship and others are ignored. Let the biblical text guide you in such evaluations.

5. *How do you promote intergenerational worship in a positive manner?* Paul writes that God has given certain gifts to individuals whose role is "to equip the saints for the work of ministry, for building up the body of Christ until all of us come to the unity in the faith and of the knowledge of the Son of God, to maturity, to the measure of the full stature of Christ" (Ephes. 4:12-13). Preparing God's people for intergenerational worship and cultivating

Evelyn

Robert Nordling

"Hello, my name is Evelyn, and I'd like to talk to you about some of the music you use on Sunday mornings."

Another complaint! The pastor had come just a few years ago, and this 100-plus-year-old church experienced dramatic change as its population grew from 90 faithful older members to over 1,000 worshipers—mostly college students. The pastor had been clear about his vision to reach out to the university just across the street. As the students poured into services, there had been frustrations all around, as we tried hard both to honor our past and to embrace our present in worship.

"What can I do for you, Evelyn?"

"Well, I'm the music leader for the seniors group that meets in the church hall on Tuesdays," she explained. "We eat lunch together, have a speaker, and then sing for a little while before an ethos to support it involve four related components—teaching, discernment, modeling, and accountability.

The congregation must be taught. The people must understand Christ's vision for the church. The congregation must be offered a biblical vision of the church. Congregants must be taught about the essence of worship. Explain why new elements are added to the worship service. If a practice is discontinued, explain why. Do not assume that people understand the reasons for change. Share stories that challenge the congregation to develop a vision for how worship ought to be.

Demonstrate discernment by graciously and patiently assessing worship practices in light of Scripture, and reflect on and adjust practices to promote an intergenerational ethos. Change is scary; take time to discern its potential impact on others. This demonstrated discernment will make what is taught more profitable and practical.

---

closing the meeting. We were wondering if we might be able to get copies of those new songs you are using in church."

"Why would you want that music, Evelyn?"

"Well, we find some of the newer music a bit challenging, and I thought that if we practiced it a bit together during our meetings on Tuesdays, we might be able to participate better on Sundays. Some of those songs seem pretty difficult—to us anyway."

I promised Evelyn the music.

In all my years of music ministry I had seldom witnessed such selfless maturity. This music would *never* be the favorite of these good people, but somehow that didn't seem to matter. Their desire to sing as active participants in worship alongside those younger worshipers allowed then to lay aside their own musical preferences in deference to others.

I learned a valuable lesson that day from Evelyn and that group of seniors.

Good leaders intentionally model what they teach. A congregation must experience how this teaching works itself out in practice. Therefore the leaders of a congregation both teach and exemplify in their own ministries what they have been teaching. People's lives are shaped by what they truly value. A leader who practices what he or she teaches reinforces the teaching and deepens the discernment.

Practice accountability to each other. Address questions and criticisms scripturally. Help people to understand the difference between personal preferences and scriptural warrant. When congregation members are invited to participate in worship, equip them for the roles they are to fill. Drawing on the body of Christ metaphor and on Paul's handling of eating meat sacrificed to idols pursues accountability in love, with respect, and in a manner that promotes spiritual maturity and unity in the faith.

6. *How can we help people contribute their gifts to worship?* The gifts the Holy Spirit has distributed within each congregation are varied in their uniqueness and diversity. Yet all are valuable, and all are needed. Do you help people discover their gifts? Are they given opportunity to develop those gifts? Can you identify the gifts available in the congregation? Do members know what their gifts are? Explore how the giftedness of God's people in your congregation ought to be celebrated. A variety of study materials are available for groups to use in discovering their gifts.

A Healthy Ethos

Worship that is genuinely intergenerational is best attempted in the context of efforts to create an entire ethos or culture of intergenerational relationships. Such an ethos will involve deep relationships that seek the good of others and require that the body work together to encourage corporate spiritual formation. It involves relationships in which people value and respect each other, regardless of age, sex, or any developmental considerations. This is an ethos grounded in Scripture and not based merely on contemporary culture.

Fostering such an ethos requires us to allow ourselves to be shaped more by the truths of Scripture and the metaphor that we are the body of Christ than by the values and pressures of our culture.

It summons us to "hold fast to the confession of our hope without wavering, for he who has promised is faithful. And let us consider how to provoke one another to love and good deeds, not neglecting to meet together, as is the habit of some, but encouraging one another, and all the more as you see the Day approaching" (Heb. 10:23-25).

Questions for Discussion

1. In the church there has been a push to pursue racial diversity. Are there similarities between pursuing racial diversity and generational diversity? Should there be an equal emphasis on generational diversity and harmony? If so, why? If not, why not?

2. Suppose that in your congregation a young mother is in need of some assistance with her infant during worship. Who—i.e., a person of what age—do you think would be most comfortable getting up to help her? Who would be most *un*comfortable helping her? What does this answer say about the church as the body of Christ?

3. Drawing on the body of Christ metaphor, discuss the relative benefits of (a) involving children in worship so that they contribute to the overall service, and (b) having them sing a song in front of the congregation once, twice, or even several times a year.

4. What values and activities in the culture of your congregation can best assist your congregation in wrestling with the differences between personal preferences and scriptural warrant as they relate to intergenerational worship? Point to two or three factors that will help the most.

5. If you were to have a robust conversation about intergenerational worship today in the congregation you attend, what kinds of considerations would be most likely to come up for discussion? Would they be helpful? How would you respond?

Darwin Glassford is currently associate professor of church education at Calvin Theological Seminary in Grand Rapids, Michigan. He previously served as professor of Bible and Christian education and assistant academic dean at Montreat College in Montreat, North Carolina. He has served in many youth settings and carries a passion for church education.

Sunday Morning Parenting

John Witvliet

Sunday mornings can be the low point in a kid's week. Tired parents hurry kids off to church, where they will count ceiling tiles during a long sermon, sit silently during much of the music, feel uncomfortable around people they don't know, and finish their allotted candy much too soon.

Sunday mornings can also be a highlight for kids, a time to sing favorite songs about God, to listen to compelling stories about what God is doing in the world, to meet a whole community of people who know and love them, and—lest we sell them short—to think thoughts about God and to pray prayers that are more profound than most of us adults would give them credit for.

Our goal, obviously, should be to move, insofar as possible, from scenario 1 to scenario 2. That takes the collaborative teamwork of parents, pastors, musicians, church-school teachers, and congregation members. To imagine what that teamwork might look like, consider the following imaginary letters. Each conveys a vision for children's full, conscious, and active participation in worship and some practical ideas for pulling that off. Not every idea suggested will work for every congregation, of course, but I hope that most congregations will find a few ideas for helping kids to worship more deeply. As you read, consider what adaptations you would make for a letter to your congregation.

Dear Parent,

We are grateful for the privilege of working with your child in our church education program. We believe that people of every generation, including our children, are vitally important members of our church. Not only can children learn from us, but we can learn from them.

We hope to incorporate children more fully into the worship life of our congregation. In our church-school classes, children are being trained to understand worship better, and we will teach them many of the songs that we sing in worship. In worship, we will work to make sure that every service has at least one element that ties in with our education program.

But we need your help. Helping kids worship is ultimately *your* job. They need encouragement to participate in worship just as much as they need encouragement in learning to read or play soccer. To help you in your role as "worship participation coaches," we've gathered suggestions from several parents about how to make worship more meaningful to children. Here is some of what we heard:

- "After church, we take home the bulletin or order of worship and use some of the same Scripture readings, prayers, and songs in our family devotions."
- "I was surprised at how young my kids were when they wanted to look up the songs in the hymnal."
- "When I get to church, I always look around for new artwork or symbols that I can explain to my kids."
- "We found some good books at a local Christian bookstore about going to church, and we read them at home on Saturday nights."
- "During the passing of the peace or welcome time, I try to start by hugging or shaking hands with my kids. It's good for me, and it helps them participate. Also, they have no problem saying 'Christ's peace be with you,' whereas I often stumble simply trying to say 'Good morning.'"
- "After church I always reward our kids when they can remember the first illustration the minister used in the sermon. It may be a little much to expect them to listen for 20 minutes or more, but having them listen for the first story or name they hear teaches them not to tune out right away."
- "Our kids always connect more in worship when we don't arrive at the last minute."
- "At my brother's church, the pastor provides a sermon outline so that the older kids can follow along and fill in the blanks. That really helps them learn to listen."

- "For our family, the offering is a big deal. The kids always put the money in the collection plate. After church, we always look up on the Internet some information about where the money is going."
- "Our kids love to sing at home, so we found some CDs and piano music of songs we sing a lot in church, and we try to learn a new song every month or so."
- "It sounds simple, but when we read a prayer or litany from the bulletin, I make sure my kids follow along as I point to the words—the same thing I do when we read books at home. We also like to take the bulletin home and use the same words later in the week."

Let us know some other tips that you've discovered. We'll keep a complete list posted on our church's Web site.

To help you further, we've assembled a series of children's books about worship in the church library. Please let us know if you have any questions about our worship services or suggestions to help us incorporate children more fully.

In Christ,
Your Pastor and Children's Ministry Committee

Dear Pastor and Members of the Children's Ministry Committee,

Thank you for all the work you are doing for our congregation. We value your leadership in programs for our children. You asked us to give some thought to our role as "worship participation coaches," so here you go.

Your point about our being worship coaches was quite a new way for us to think about Sunday. We're so eager for an hour simply to rest a bit from everything, that we've left our kids' participation mostly up to you. The extra effort you ask from us will take some adjustments.

Sunday morning is a big challenge for us as parents. We do our best to get everyone organized and out the door in time for church. But with working the night shift and keeping all the kids' activities organized, we usually pull into the church parking lot during the first song. I guess I do have to admit, however, that we're almost never late for gymnastics class on Saturdays. We'll have to prioritize church a little more.

On vacation this summer we visited a church that changed the "children's moment" in worship from a mini-sermon to a prayer time. We really appreciated that. Our kids never really get the point of a lot of children's sermons, even though we kind of like them ourselves. When we ask them after church what the children's sermon was about, they say things like, "It was about a flashlight," or "It was about a bag with something in it." By having a special prayer time with the kids, you give us something we can repeat at home. And they really seem to sense the difference between being talked at and being led in prayer. They learn so many lessons in school all week, but there are never enough opportunities to learn to pray.

Having said that, we think that what you want is for our kids to participate not just in "the children's moment" but also in other parts of the service. Would it be too much to ask to have one song, one sermon reference, and one prayer item every week be kid-specific? We noticed that one of our guest pastors prayed for kids who worried about bullies on the playground and then used a sermon illustration about going to gym class in the middle of the school day. Our kids sat right up when they heard that. And we certainly have enough good songs in church school that we could sing one of them in worship each week.

One problem for our kids in worship is the lack of repetition. I know we do a lot of the same stuff every week, but the stories, songs, and prayers change all the time. At home our kids love to hear their favorite books over and over. When we sing songs at home, even when we learn a new one, the kids won't let us stop singing until we've sung our favorites. Could we take some basic songs and prayers and use them regularly in worship for a season at a time? Perhaps the Lord's Prayer would be a good place to start. We could say it every Sunday of Advent, for example. And could we also use the Bible verses the kids are learning in their church-school classes? Psalm 23 or 100 or John 3:16 would be good for all of us to say in worship. If we did this, perhaps we could get a note in the bulletin to prompt us to work at using that text at home throughout the week too.

In closing, we want to add that while we long deeply for child-*friendly* worship, we're not interested in having worship that is child-*centered*, as if the other generations weren't important. And we certainly don't want worship that is child*ish*. Our kids need practices to grow into. They spend much of their lives with people their own age. Worship is one of the few times they connect with people of all ages. We hope that never changes.

Thanks for taking the time to think about our kids!

Sincerely,
Appreciative Parents

John Witvliet teaches theology, worship, and music at Calvin College and Calvin Theological Seminary in Grand Rapids, Michigan, directs the Calvin Institute of Christian Worship, and is the father of four children under 6 years old, including a set of triplets. This material first appeared in The Banner *(Faith Alive Christian Resources), the official publication of the Christian Reformed Church, in 2007 and is used by permission.*

CHAPTER 6

The Power of Telling a Story

Jeff Barker

The telling of stories has great power. However, people in our culture tell stories to each other far less than people in other cultures and in previous generations. Jeff Barker is convinced that we've lost something precious in the process of doing less storytelling. If we learn to tell stories more often, and particularly in our worship, we will bind the generations together in multiple ways—by teaming together to tell the stories, by jointly listening, and by sharing the remembrance of God's acts.

It is significant that God does not present us with salvation in the form of an abstract truth, or a precise definition or a catchy slogan, but as *story*.

—from Eugene Peterson's *The Message,*
"Introduction to Exodus"[1]

If God longs for young and old to come to worship together, what will we do when we get there? One thing we will do is tell stories. The best stories have power that is long and high and deep. I call story's power *long* because at age 10 and age 50 I have been hooked by this sentence: "The woman bore a son, and called his name Samson, and the child grew." I call story's power *high* because no matter how tall I am, this sentence will always look me in the eye: "Let the one who is without sin throw the first stone." I call story's power *deep* because no matter how far I dig, I will never get to the bottom of the mystery of the Ananias and Sapphira story.

All of the Bible stories I've just mentioned might be called "adult stories": they have sex, violence, and death. But I remember my dad reading me the story of Samson when I was a first-grader, and I loved it. Great stories cut across the boundaries of age, and if we tell them when the church family gathers, they will bind us. They will bind us in common experience when the characters and events creep into our conversations. They will bind us in common values as together we laugh and gasp at the follies and victories in these stories. They will bind us in love and respect as we sit together, seeing with each other's eyes and hearing with each other's ears. This binding power happens throughout the general culture with stories from television, the newspaper, the Internet, or film, but in the general culture, there is a dividing of worlds—generations brought into being by hearing separate stories. We can affirm this generational division within worship, or we can change it with the simple but profound power of telling a story, a common story, week after week.

If we are to pursue this path, we must provide the time within the worship plan, choose the stories wisely, and tell them well. These things can and should be done. The intergenerational church should be a storytelling church.

Arlene

About a year ago, I met an 83-year-old woman named Arlene Schuiteman. She's 30 years older than I, so I guess you could say we're from different generations. She lives just a few miles away, and I went to visit her because I was told she had a story. Arlene told me about her time as a missionary nurse among the Nuer people in the village of Nasir in southern Sudan. She lived there eight years. An old man named Yuol became a Christian while she was there, but he was one of only a few. In 1963 Arlene was suddenly expelled by the Sudanese government, never able to return. She arrived back in the United States confused and defeated. She wondered what she had accomplished with those eight years of her life.

One Sunday, 40 years after she had left the Sudan, Arlene was invited to worship with a group of Sudanese refugees in nearby Sioux Falls, South Dakota. At the end of the service, Arlene introduced herself. Some of the people were shocked to hear her name. They were the grown children of people Arlene had cared for on the banks of the Sobat River all those years before. They told Arlene that the village was now full of Christians. Arlene felt as if she'd gotten a glimpse into heaven. I sat at the small kitchen table in the little brick house Arlene's parents had built when they moved off the farm into Sioux Center, Iowa, and I asked her if she'd let me develop her story into a play.

We previewed the play *Sioux Center Sudan*[2] in front of Arlene and her family and friends. It was a great day, surrounded with prayer and sweat. Then we took the play on tour and, two months later, brought the story home. That Sunday evening in Sioux Center, the church was jammed with over a thousand people. The congregation included Vandy, Arlene's dear friend from Pennsylvania (and the author of the book *A Leopard Tamed,* which tells of Vandy's Bible translation work while living in Nasir). Dr. Bob Gordon, Arlene's Sudan medical supervisor, was brought by his son from a nursing home on the other side of Iowa. Several Sudanese natives had traveled from as far away as Georgia. One Sudanese man stood up after the play and said, "I want you to think of the most famous movie star you know. Think of what it would be like to meet that person. That's how we feel being here tonight and meeting Nya Bigoaa and Nyarial (as Arlene and Vandy are known in Africa). And Dr. Bob. We have heard about them all our growing-up years. We are Christians today because of what they did for us."

After the play Arlene wrote me a thank-you note that included this phrase from Psalm 71: "Even when I am old and gray, do not forsake me, O God, till I declare your power to the next generation, your might to all who are to come" (NIV). Arlene looked into the faces of those college students portraying her story, and she saw God's answer to the Psalmist's prayer and her own. It was for this that Arlene had told her story, satisfying a deep need for her, filling her with gratitude and joy, and encouraging the entire community. Arlene believed that God had sent her to Africa in the first place to declare the power of God to the next generation. It was a holy calling. Now, by sharing her story, her calling was continuing.

Stories Declare the Power of God

What does it means to declare the power of God to the next generation? What is the power of God? What is meant by "declare?" Who is the next generation? Why is this transaction important? How does this happen in the church? I don't mean to make more of Psalm 71 than the Scripture intends, but this text and its context can serve as a guide to a great treasure for worshiping Christians of all ages—a treasure that is now being reclaimed within many of our worship centers. That treasure is story.

Start with the power of God. *Almighty. Omnipotent. Supreme.* To say the name of God is to announce majesty. One of our worshipful tasks is to reposition ourselves by stating that God is God and we are not. Worship is realignment. This simple act of naming brings balance and sanity to our human journey. But it's not enough. The declaration of a truth begs for an example. That example is a "for instance," a deed, an event, an action—a story! It is not enough simply to stand up and state, "Our God is omnipotent." If we do, some child (or child in the faith) will say, "Prove it." Or "Tell it!" They want to hear the story.

"Now there arose a new king over Egypt, who did not know Joseph. And he said to his people, 'Behold the people of Israel are too many and too mighty for us.'" *Story.*

"And there came out from the camp of the Philistines a champion named Goliath, of Gath. . . . He stood and shouted. . . . 'Choose a man for yourselves and let him come down to me.'" *Story.*

"On the first day of the week, at early dawn, they went to the tomb, taking the spices which they had prepared." *Story.*

"Now as he journeyed he approached Damascus, and suddenly a light from heaven flashed around him. And he fell to the ground and heard a voice saying to him, 'Saul, Saul, why do you persecute me?'" *Story.*

The power of God is cradled in a basket made of bulrushes. It's in five smooth stones lying on the bottom of a brook. It's in the echoing air of an empty grave. It's in the scales that fall from the eyes.

If we are to comprehend and celebrate the power of God (or any facet of God's character), a story is a reasonable request. I can't help thinking that when David wrote, "till I declare your power," he was talking of telling stories. If you back up a couple of verses, you'll find, "I will come and proclaim your mighty acts," and "to this day I declare your marvelous deeds." How would David proclaim those mighty acts or declare those marvelous deeds without telling stories?

Storytelling was not a new idea with David. Perhaps his father, Jesse, had raised him under the practice of Deuteronomy 6:20-21: "When your children ask you in time to come, 'What is the mean-

Sharing the Bible Story

Jeff Barker

A pastor recently invited our touring theater ensemble to perform at a noon Lenten service, attended mostly by senior adults. I explained that we didn't have any short plays on the Passion of Jesus. Would he accept an Old Testament story? He agreed.

When we arrived, the woman who ran the preschool that met in the church building asked, "May I bring the children to watch the play?" I said, "It's the story of Elisha and the chariots of fire. We speak directly from the King James. And someone gets killed in the story." She said, "Well, whatever you decide is what we'll do." I said, "Bring the kids."

At noon exactly, the kids marched single file into the second row. The senior saints were scattered out behind them. I sat off to the side of the children, watching them. I saw them slide forward and hang their chins on the back of the pew in front of them, eyes glued to those moving images. They never made a sound.

The choice to include the children was doubly confirmed when I ate lunch with the seniors and heard them delighting over the presence of those kids.

I'd like to see everyone go to work to return these profound family stories to the sanctuary, in a way that is better than a droning reader with nose buried in the book. When restored to their original performance tradition, these stories open their arms to every generation.

ing of the decrees and the statutes and the ordinances that the Lord
our God has commanded you?' then you shall say to your children, 'We were Pharaoh's slaves in Egypt. But the Lord brought
us out of Egypt with a mighty hand.'" In other words, when your
kids want to know why we practice this religion, tell them the old
stories.

Storytelling had a strong tradition from generation to generation among the Israelites, and that practice was reclaimed in Ref-
ormation worship. John Witvliet reminds us that "Nearly every
major work on the meaning and purpose of liturgy written by a
prominent Reformed theologian has emphasized the memorializ-
ing function of liturgy, the way it recounts divine action in the past
in ways that anticipate divine action in the future."[3] This storytelling refrain sings through the first chapter of "Worship Seeking
Understanding," as Witvliet quotes other thinkers about worship:

Nicholas Wolterstorff: "A striking feature of the Christian liturgy is that it is focused not just on God's nature but on God's
actions; and more specifically on actions which took place in historical time."[4]

Hughes Oliphant Old: "That God acts in history is fundamental to our theology; that we rejoice in these mighty acts is fundamental to our worship."[5]

Witvliet concludes that "one criterion to apply to worship in
any congregation, regardless of the liturgical style it embraces, is
that of historical remembrance and proclamation: Does worship
proclaim the whole sweep of divine activity past, present, and future?"[6]

What stories of God at work are we talking about? Well, what
about Bible stories? In fact, let's resuscitate that phrase "Bible stories." Many of us have heard that term so often in conjunction
with children's education that we no longer think that Bible stories
are for all ages—a terrible shame. Let's tell Bible stories when all
the congregation is present. In fact, I'll be so bold as to propose
that we've lost enough ground that we should tell at least one
Bible story pretty much every time we get together for worship.
This idea of the whole congregation's getting together and listening to the same story is crucial to the meaning of story (and to the
meaning of this book). Stories are experienced in various ways,

depending on who's listening. After sitting through the run of several nights of the same play (an experience I've had many times after decades of directing), I know that the makeup of the audience changes the play. And after years of leading two identical worship services on Sunday mornings, I can attest that the experience is different when the makeup is more seniors (our early service) or more college students and young families (our later service). My point here is to say that we will all do well to hear the Bible's stories not only through our own ears but through the ears of those to whose generation we do not belong.

One of the beautiful things about stories is that the best ones function across generations. The event structure of a story, like falling dominoes, attracts and holds everyone's attention, even young children's, while the values housed within a protagonist's conflicting motivations provide nuance and mystery for those most experienced in life. Stories are such fundamental tools for living that half the Bible is full of them. Bible stories are for everyone.

There are threats to the plan to reclaim Bible stories for worship, and one of these is worth addressing immediately. For the sake of saving time in the worship hour, we are tempted to tell *about* Bible stories without actually *telling* them. We may assume that those who have previously heard or read the stories will be content with an allusion. Why repeat what they already know? We settle for the *idea* of the story rather than *the story itself*. I'm not opposed to scriptural allusion that creates harmony within the acts of worship, but as a song thrives on the heartbeat of its melody, liturgy needs story. Some of those present are young in age or young in experience with the Bible. They don't yet know the whole story.[7] If all they get is allusion, that's empty to them; they come away empty-hearted. As for those who already know the stories, good stories bear repeating—again and again. We experience this truth with our own family stories. When we get together, we find ourselves saying, "Remember the time you . . . ," and everyone grins, knowing what's coming. The repetition of our stories is part of what binds us to each other and to the values that shape us.

Let us tell the stories. All of them. We have a book full.

But let's not stop with Bible stories, because God's work does not stop there. If our worship is to include, as Witvliet suggests,

Eight-Year-Olds Listen Too!

Eleazar Merriweather

At St. Luke's Church, we believe that true Christian worship is both traditional and contemporary—simultaneously—like the "head" and "tail" of the same coin. So we are free to change our practices of worship without feeling that we are compromising principles.

Our primary focus is what we bring to it rather than what we receive out of it.

One Sunday, I received great encouragement from a young girl.

During the Lenten season our worship leaders presented a drama of the Passover story so that all ages would be able to live into it. We knew we had engaged them all when an eight-year-old girl said to her parents afterward, "I needed to go to the restroom so bad . . . but I would not because I did not want to miss any of the play. It was really good and I learned a lot."

Yes, eight-year-olds participate too. We ought not to sell them short.

"the whole sweep of divine activity," then we should tell stories of God at work today, in your congregation and mine. The Arlene Schuitemans of all our churches are waiting for the answer to David's prayer in their own lives. "Even when I am old and gray, do not forsake me, O God, till I declare your power to the next generation, your might to all who are to come" (Ps. 71:18 NIV). The Arlenes are waiting to tell, and the next generation is waiting to hear. The stories of God at work in the lives of our people are the unclaimed diamonds of the church.

√ Restoring Our Stories

How did we lose the power of telling Bible stories and our own stories within worship? Let me be quick to affirm that not every congregation has lost its story. Some worshiping traditions have continued the practice of testimony,[8] and recently, there has been afoot in the church significant encouragement to reclaim the orality of Scripture.[9] Nevertheless much restorative work remains to be done. How did we get here? How is it that many Christian worshipers can go to church Sunday after Sunday without hearing a present witness to God's work? I'm quite certain that you have your own answers. I speak at this point not with authority but as one who is wondering about this question myself. Here are some possible considerations.

1. *Did we overemphasize music?* The emphasis on music became so great during the 20th century that for some the word "worship" became synonymous with music. A friend of mine wrote in an e-mail conversation about worship, "You sound as if you think that worship includes the sermon." *Hmmm.* When we adjusted the liturgy at our church to include a bit less music and a bit more story, my daughter said to me, "I like the changes, but I wish we could worship more." I said, "You mean you wish there was more singing?" Yep.

2. *Before music was so emphasized, the Bible was the central emphasis of worship.* It wasn't so much Bible story as it was a Bible text in support of propositional preaching to help us live godly lives. This sounds pretty good, but many of our preachers have learned to save time—going straight to the lesson of the story by dispensing with the story itself.[10]

3. *I wonder if we got too proud for testimonies.* Did we fear some kind of pride?—not obvious pride, but perhaps the sort of false humility that says, "My story isn't important." Or maybe a stuffiness that says, "Isn't testimony a quaint remnant of pietism?"

4. *Some of the longing for story has been filled by the fictional slice-of-life sketch.* I'm certainly not opposed to the power of a fictional story, but did this dramatic model usurp the time available for testimonies and Bible stories?

5. *Maybe we've become lazy.* It's work to prepare stories for a public gathering. Are we willing to invest the time and effort to prepare well?

6. *Maybe we are we afraid of those who will abuse this activity* by turning Bible stories into inauthentic performances, and by making personal stories into opportunities for attention to self.

7. *It could be that we have we tried to include too much Scripture* without stopping to ask, "Do we have a regular diet of complete Bible stories in our worship?"

8. *The Bible got printed up as a book.* That was a wonderful thing. But it may have led us to believe that the Bible was always a book, meant to be read rather than told.[11]

All right, you get the point that there are many factors. Some of us will need to go on a bit of a journey to return the power of story to worship.

Where shall we start if we are to go on this journey of restoring the power of story? I'm convinced that we should start with Bible stories and testimonies. But please just relax, because I'm not going to advocate that everyone should create theater performances out of the biblical text or from the lives of the people in your church. If you have those skills and resources, that's great, but the power of story is available wherever two or three are gathered, regardless of your performance training.

Bible Stories

Start with a single person who memorizes and tells the story. That simple step—the lifting of the face from the page—will work wonders. And kids can memorize like gangbusters. High-school and college students are also great memorizers, and many of them are secure enough to get the attention off themselves when they're telling the story. Indeed, with a little encouragement, every generation can get involved. Assign Bible stories for worship, and go to work. That will keep you going for years and years. It's not new or clever; it's classic and deep.

There is tremendous power in the individual storyteller, but it is possible and sometimes desirable to have a group involved.[12] Here's the most simple version: assign two verses to each person, and have the individuals stand in a line and pass the microphone down. Notice this: Bible stories include lots of dialogue and action, and a group can help everyone hear those multiple voices. I've come to believe that this is not a clever overlay on the Bible. It's a reclamation of the performance values built into these ancient texts that grew out of oral cultures. Find the characters in the story, and assign the parts. Then you can present the story as a Reader's Theatre—or in a full staging with tableaux, tribal drums, and singers! [13]

Personal Stories

Alongside the telling of Bible stories, we tell our own stories. It's not either/or; it's both/and. As I've said earlier, some traditions don't need coaching in this area, but for some, testimony is a lost experience. Consider this: ask someone in your congregation to share a "God at Work in My Life" moment in an upcoming worship service. Here's what I say when I invite someone to do this: "Would you be willing to share a very brief story on Sunday about God at work in your life? If so, I'll ask you to write it out and share it with me a few days in advance. When you speak it aloud, be sure that it times out to be three minutes or less. As for content, it can be about the story of your faith journey, or it can be from a single day in your life. Try to include at least one Bible verse. Oh, and please come to church early so you can practice with the microphone in the space and find out what your cue is." My experience has been that many, many people are willing to do this, once they've seen it done a couple of times.

Another effective way of sharing stories is by using brief verbal snapshots. The first time I experienced this method, Karen, my wife and colleague, and I were at a gathering of missionaries some years ago. We told the group that we wished we could see all their slides. Because that was impossible, we asked them each to take five minutes and write down an image of somewhere they had been that past year. We asked them to take themselves back to that location and to stand in a single place as a human camera, recording sights and sound as well as their own feelings. We told them to keep the account to one brief paragraph. Here's one of the amazing "slides" from the slideshow we had that night.

Nyadeng, a disheveled young Sudanese mother, is pausing under a Tamarind tree in the early afternoon heat. She wearily supports her one-year-old daughter on her left hip, and with the right hand clings to her five-year-old son. Tears stream down her face. There is no wind. Shimmering heat rises from the dirt road in a wave of lonely lethargy. Behind Nyadeng, at the edge of the tree's shadow, is the carcass of an armored personnel carrier. Its door is ajar; its tires are flat. Patches of rust indicate that its life in the war zone is complete. But for Nyadeng, the horror of the war zone will never die. Back up the road, she has just abandoned her three-year-old daughter, who was too big to carry and too little to run. Nyadeng has left her, hoping to run fast enough and far enough to keep her two remaining children alive.[14]

And sometimes these "slides" or snapshots can be harvested spontaneously in worship. This method works in congregations large and small. One Sunday our pastor was preaching on the first half of Acts 9, a story that begins with Saul's conversion and that ends with his finally making it safely home to Tarsus. At the start of the service, I took a microphone into the congregation and asked, "Has anyone ever been stranded somewhere and couldn't get home?" Hands went up, and I brought the microphone. We heard stories of weather problems, car problems, and troubles caused by the events of September 11, 2001. This part took about three minutes. Then I said, "Later in today's worship service, we're going to hear about a man in the Bible who was stuck away from home." That theme of journeying toward home served as the guide to our entire service, culminating, as you might have guessed, with "Maranatha . . . Come, Lord Jesus!"

Congregational Stories

As each church member has a story, each congregation also has a story. For the 75th anniversary celebration of our congregation, Karen thumbed through old consistory minutes and put together a Reader's Theatre piece. Those quotations from the minutes told a fascinating, hilarious, poignant, and healing story of God at work over the years in our home church.

There are stories everywhere. In addition to our storybook, the Bible, and our own family stories in our local church, we may also find appropriate stories from the culture at large. And although we should never overlook telling stories when we are gathered together, we may find creative ways to tell stories to one another when we are apart. Our pastor is currently on sabbatical, and he has made it easy to keep up with him via his blog.

In worship, we celebrate God's work in history as well as today. We also yearn toward God's future work. We affirm the story that is to come. Here's something to try. After any presentation of the Scripture, readers in some traditions say, "The Word of the Lord," and the worshipers respond in unison, "Thanks be to God." If your congregation is not locked into that tradition, it may sometimes be appropriate for the biblical storyteller to close the book, or take a step closer, or somehow make it clear that the story is over, and then look us in the eye and say slowly and securely, "God did it once!" And we respond (with pretty loud voices), "He'll do it again!" Do you see what I'm getting at? We, in the present, listen to the past and affirm our hopes of God's action in the future. That's good worship theology. And it's a joy.[15]

Consider this starting goal: one Bible story or one personal testimony told somewhere in half of your worship gatherings. At first, it may seem impossible to find the time. After you include one story on just a few occasions, it will become much easier because its value will become clear. That which is treasured is protected. And that which binds generations together is doubly treasured.

The Next Generation

Who is "the next generation" mentioned in Psalm 71? It's simple. The next generation comprises those who will live longer than I do. If the next generation knows the stories of God at work in my life, then the stories have a chance of outliving me. It's a little miracle, this resurrection of God's work through the power of telling a story. The enemy of our souls would be happier if those stories died with us. A pastor recently told me that the mission program

An Intergenerational Study

Jan Zuidema

Several years ago, in an attempt to help our youth understand the drama of worship better, we used some interactive materials designed to help the students see worship as story. We studied these materials during the usual education hour after the morning worship service. However, in the process of preparing for these meetings, we came to realize that these materials offered a unique opportunity to help both our youth and their parents. With that in mind, we invited not only our students but also their parents to some roundtable discussions on successive Sunday mornings. Then we also decided to make this a true intergenerational opportunity and invited the entire congregation to attend.

Groups met in a large room at round tables, with the chairs at each table marked "student" or "adult," so the various ages sat together for each session. Each week the group was introduced to a part of the worship service. Students, their parents, and other members of the congregation were able to discuss why it is important each week to hear God calling us, to tell him we're sorry, to hear his word for our lives, to be washed and fed through the sacraments, and, finally, to be sent out to be a blessing.

Beyond understanding worship better, all of us got to know and understand each other better. Participants realized that we don't all fit the usual stereotypes of our age groups. The class served to foster a better relationship between our students and the wider church community, helping to move us further along the path to truly becoming one as the body of Christ.

in his church caught fire after the play *Sioux Center Sudan* was performed there. When I told Arlene, she said, "Oh, I remember that church. The students were so disappointed after performing there because there weren't very many in attendance and the response seemed indifferent." Then she said, "Do you ever sense that there is spiritual warfare happening during the play?" I admitted that I may not be sensitive enough to such things. Arlene said, "Well, I just use it as encouragement to pray."

After the first year's tour of *Sioux Center Sudan*, Arlene called my office for an appointment. She sat across from me and asked if I would be interested in writing another story, a story about the years she spent in Ethiopia and then Zambia. She doesn't know how many more years she has before the stories will die with her. In regard to our own stories, you and I don't either. Which stories do we take the time to tell? God has not given us the problem of too few stories to tell but, rather, too many.

Arlene represents a host of people in our congregations with a host of stories waiting to be told, stories that will hold us together as generations and increase our understanding of each other. Which of their stories will be told, and how will they get told? Who will ask the right questions so that their stories are told to at least one person? Then who will decide if and when and how their stories are told in worship that so that we can celebrate what God is doing now, where we live?

We live in an era of the cult of the famous. The mythology of this cult says that the most important stories are those known by the most people. The doctrine of this cult is that you must pay attention to the new (which comes to us daily as "the news"). The national news, says the cult, is more important than the local news, and the local news is more important than the neighborhood news.

The church has fallen prey to this cult if we undervalue God's work with a dozen rough folk in our own little Nazareth. God has not fallen prey to the cult of the famous, and God still cares to work in each home and church. These local stories are newsworthy. Who will make room for their telling and hearing? I've been cheered to witness some churches pushing back against the cult of the famous by creating what they call "refrigerator art." These are songs and stories that are not purchased through the major publishers. They are worship art created locally, like the pictures every child gives his or her parent to put on the family fridge. I find much value in this impulse.

I often remember my first time sitting at Arlene's little kitchen table. How could she have trusted me to hear and then retell her story? When I first met her, she was reticent, and she needed to know that I actually wanted to hear her story. At each stage of the journey, a relationship of trust had to be built and maintained. This task of trust-building is the foundation upon which storytelling is built. These trusting relationships are what our congregations should be known for. This trust is the discipline to which we are all assigned. We meet and get to know one another as brothers and sisters in the body of Christ. We develop friendships, and out of those friendships we build the trust that leads to story prompts: Where were you baptized? How have you experienced God's call in your life? Have you ever seen a miracle? The answers to those questions, however they are gleaned, are stories of God at work, and they should be spoken in each local church for the benefit of every generation.

> O God, from my youth, you have taught me,
> and I still proclaim your wondrous deeds.
> So even to old age and gray hairs,
> Do not forsake me, O God,
> till I declare your power
> to the next generation,
> your might to all who are to come.
>   —Psalm 71:18 NIV

For Discussion

Try something. Take three minutes to write an image of a time when you knew you wanted to follow Jesus all your life. Write about the very first thing that comes to mind. Get going right away. Include time of day and place. Take yourself back there and describe in concrete language what you see, hear and feel. Here's an example:

> It is Saturday late at night. I am 13 years old. I am alone in my bedroom. I just got home from summer camp, where I heard a speaker describe the terrible pain of crucifixion. And I'm thinking, "That was my fault." And I am crying.

Then sign it. I might sign this as, "Jeff Barker, now a college professor, age 52." Now just read them around the circle.

Jeff Barker has been a theater professor at Northwestern College in Orange City, Iowa, since 1988. He is the author of many plays and regularly involves his students in the process of both writing and producing his plays. In 2006 he was selected as the Iowa Professor of the Year by the Carnegie Foundation for the Advancement of Teaching. He has been a worship leader for many years and leads a student touring group which performs worship dramas, including stories verbatim from the Old Testament.

CHAPTER 7

The Power of Preaching to All Ages

Timothy Brown

Alongside the music, the sermon has been frequently maligned as a divider of the generations. How can a sermon possibly be made accessible for all ages? Is it even a goal within reach? We might expect that if someone claims this can be accomplished, the advice would come in the form of some brand-new techniques and methods. However, from his wide experience as a preacher, a student of preaching, and a teacher of homiletics, Tim Brown reaffirms some age-old convictions with a fresh new approach.

Let me get this straight; you expect me to preach a sermon for 20 minutes that will inform, persuade, and delight everyone from an 80-year-old with a hearing problem to an eight-year-old *with a hearing problem*. Thanks a lot!

This protest, of course, is the tough test that every parish preacher faces Sunday in and Sunday out, from Poughkeepsie to Portland. So who is seated in the pews as the preacher stands to proclaim the gospel on any given Sunday? If I close my eyes I can see them all now.

A 15-year-old high school sophomore doesn't seem to be listening because of the iPod earpiece in her ear. Before she was dragged to church against her will, she took one last look in the bathroom mirror and rehearsed the same litany of shame that she sounds every morning before she merges into the rush-hour traffic of her local high school: "I am not cool enough! I am not popular enough! And I am definitely not skinny enough!" She is a victim of her generational context. How will you preach to her, preacher?

A 41-year-old certified stay-at-home mom is looking back at you blankly. It isn't anything personal though—it's just that yesterday she watched her last baby turn his mortarboard tassel toward an exciting tomorrow (which doesn't include her for the most part), and the lump in her throat and the tear in her eye as she shrinks in his rearview mirror is most definitely the filter through which today's sermon will be heard. She's a victim of her generational context. How will you preach to her, preacher?

In the last pew an 89-year-old man, riddled with a series of small but debilitating strokes, sits in a wheelchair just as he does every other day of his meager life in the local nursing home. Each morning, after he does his devotions, he fingers through the obituaries of the local newspaper, disappointed again that he isn't listed there and wondering how come people 15 years younger than he get to die and he doesn't. He's a victim of his generational context. How will you preach to him, preacher?

Sprinkled throughout the sanctuary are children, teeming hordes of little ones, some of them busy with coloring books, some of them crying, and all of them bracing themselves for the avalanche of minutes they have to endure before the minister says the sorts of things that suggest to their tiny ears that the end is in sight. When the pipe organ or praise band fires up the last song, signaling that their redemption is near, they prepare to bolt for the doors like prisoners set free. They are victims of their generational context. How will you preach to them, preacher?

There are other questions the preacher must ask before he or she steps into the middle of these pulsing needs, but this one must surely be among them: How do I preach to people from such a broad range of generations, people with such divergent life experiences and needs? And this growling question is neither easily answered nor willing to stand down. Fail to answer it before you preach, however, and you can pretty much plan on a world of frustration while you are preaching.

One of the most important theologians from the early days of the Christian movement was Augustine of Hippo. Impeccably trained as a rhetorician in the ancient way of Cicero and wonderfully converted to Christ amid a tsunami of personal conflict, he was eager to combine his learning and his passion to help the preachers of his day communicate the gospel effectively in the rapidly changing social contexts of the fourth and fifth centuries. He wrote a book toward the end of the fourth century—literally with barbarians beating at the door—which outlined how he thought the Bible could be thoughtfully interpreted and engagingly proclaimed to a wide range of people who probably didn't want to hear. The book was titled *De Doctrina Christiana*, or *On Christian Teaching*. My reading in the field of preaching convinces me that every book about preaching written since—at least the ones worth reading—has had Augustine as a conversation partner. Here is how he introduces that book: "There are two things on which all interpretation of scripture depends: the process of discovering what we need to learn, and the process of presenting what we have learnt."[1] This is simple to say, but not easy to accomplish. For Augustine, preaching was like one of those doors with two-way hinges that you often see in restaurant kitchens that allow the door to swing freely in or out. Intergenerational preaching is something like those doors. The interpretive process swings in ("the process of discovering what we need to learn"), and it swings out ("the process of presenting what we have learned"). If the preacher fails to walk through the door in either direction, the sermon that he or she preaches will probably be met with a yawn. I have a serious hunch that Augustine has given us an important clue to effective intergenerational preaching.

The Door Swings In: Discovering What We Are to Learn

To Augustine's way of thinking, and to mine, the preacher who wants to have the widest intergenerational appeal in his or her preaching will draw deeply and creatively from the most intergenerational resource we have available to us—the Bible. The Scriptures themselves witness to this intergenerational dynamic at the very beginning of Israel's life in the promise land:

Hear, O Israel: The Lord is our God, the Lord alone. You shall love the Lord your God with all your heart, and with all your soul, and with all your might. Keep these words that I am commanding you today in your heart. Recite them to your children.

—Deuteronomy 6:4-7

The Scriptures were intended for Israel and Israel's children, and for us and our children too. Preachers must do today what preachers have done for centuries: hide the Word deeply in their hearts and share it as liberally as they can. In one of the initial lectures in my "Introduction to Preaching" course, I take a careful look with my students at the kind of sermon Peter preached on the Temple Mount on that first Pentecost. Obviously *what he said* is of critical importance to us, but *how he said it* should be too. If you just do the math, the number of words in the sermon, as we are given it in Acts 2:14b-36, is 510. What is more interesting, however, is that of the 510 words of the sermon, 222 of them are direct Old Testament quotations—Joel 2:28-32 in its entirety, later a smaller excerpt from Psalm 16, and then still another excerpt from Psalm 110. Roughly 46 percent of the sermon was a simple retelling of the biblical witness. And what is even more curious is that Peter's inclination after he recites the passage is not to explain it. Rather he offers it to the people as though it explained them and the crazy circumstance that they found themselves in. This is what I want to see in preaching; long, luxuriating experiences in the Word so that all who are gathered on that occasion have the time and the space to be interpreted by it. In her lovely book on preaching Barbara Brown Taylor says about the Bible:

The Bible is my birth certificate and my family tree, but it is more: it is the living vein that connects me to my maker, pumping me the stories I need to know about who we have been to one another from the beginning of time, and who we are now, and who we shall be when time is no more.[2]

In 1978 some friends of my wife and me invited us to a play at the DeWitt Theatre on the campus of Hope College in Holland, Michigan. It was a two-act performance of the Gospel of Mark by a talented British actor whose name I have long since forgotten. The impact of the performance, however, lives on. I sat mesmerized throughout the evening and thought to myself, "If an actor will do this for five dollars a head, shouldn't a pastor do it simply for the love of the congregation?" Little did I know that that night

Worship in Malawi

Edward Seely

Morning worship in Malawi lasted about two hours and 45 minutes. Cane mats were laid on the concrete floor between the first pews and the slightly raised chancel. The littlest children sat on the mats, and older children, teens, young adults, and adults sat on pews.

Four choirs—women, young women, young men, and children—occupied the front rows of pews. At various times during the worship service, each of the choral groups stood and sang to the accompaniment of two electronic keyboards played by two young men.

The children on the mats sat quietly for most of the service. When the congregation stood to sing, dance, and bring the offering to the chancel, the children also stood up and participated. They were permitted to move around as they had need and even to walk outside the building, but they always promptly and unobtrusively returned to their places on the mats. After a couple of hours, the children became a bit restless, and when some of the smallest children needed a corrective reminder, it was gently offered by either one of the women choir members, one of the elders, or an older peer sitting near them.

The children were well behaved and exhibited no sign of discontent or disruption, even during the 45-minute sermon. Their presence reminded us of God's covenant with all his children, of the pleasure they give to God and the rest of us in worship, of what they were able to learn by being with adults, and of the way they can feel at home in the corporate worship of the church.

would be the beginning of a homiletical project that would send me, and a generation of students after me, all over the world communicating as much of the Scriptures as possible to the ears of the faithful. For more than two hours that night I thrilled to the story of Jesus' Galilean evocations and his stunning Jerusalem provocations.[3] It was as though I was there, *right there*, in the company of the 12 disciples. And, if our best theologians have it right, I was in their company—or at least the Leader of the Twelve was with me and everyone else gathered that night. The Risen Christ made good on his promise to come to us through the Word. This is the staggering claim that Karl Barth made a generation ago: "God's faithfulness to the Church consists in Him making use of His freedom to come to us in His Word, and in reserving to Himself the freedom to do this again and again."[4] And this is the way that the great Jewish theologian and philosopher Abraham Heschel spoke of the Word in his important book *God in Search of Man*: "Irrefutably, indestructibly, never wearied by time, the Bible wanders through the ages, giving itself with ease to all."[5] If Heschel is right about the Bible, then we who are called to preach across the generations must speak it into the hearts and minds of every generation. If the Bible was conceived by a God who is to be worshiped and loved from one generation to another, then it must be inherently intergenerational. If we simply let the Bible speak for itself, it will necessarily speak to all generations.

Two of our five grandchildren live just around the corner from us. This, of course, is a grandparent's dream world. From time to time I have the privilege of going down and putting them to bed. A while ago, I was putting seven-year-old Thaddaeus to bed following the usual drill: serve a treat, go to the bathroom to wash hands, and then climb into bed for a story. It so happens that Thaddaeus's favorite bedtime story is Margery Williams's *The Velveteen Rabbit,* but on this night his copy was nowhere to be found. Thaddie's frustration grew with each passing minute, and so did mine. Nothing else would satisfy his bedtime reading interests. Dr. Seuss? No! *Winnie the Pooh?* No! Nothing was going to work tonight except *The Velveteen Rabbit!* Then, by divine inspiration, I asked him if I could tell him a story that I would make up. (I wasn't being completely honest about the making-it-up part, as you will see in just a minute, but I wanted him to buy into my plan.) Not wanting to hurt my feelings, he responded with a doleful "OK." We climbed into bed, and I told him he should probably let me hug him tight because the story I was going to tell him had strange characters in it. His interest was piqued. And then I began reciting for him the amazing worship scene from the fourth and fifth chapters of the Apocalypse of St. John. Thaddie liked it a lot. He liked it so much that when I was done he said, "Bumpa, it was like Jesus was in my bedroom! Do it again!" And I did do it again. I learned that night what Barth meant by God's reserving the right to come to us again and again through his Word. And I also learned that night just how intergenerational the Scriptures really are.

The Door Swings Out: Presenting What We Have Learned

Now back to our original question: "How are you going to preach to all these different people?" At the very least, I hope that when we all preach we are not "tedious to listen to, difficult to understand, and, finally, disagreeable to believe." Those great words belong to the same book on preaching by St. Augustine to which I referred earlier. Look with me at a larger excerpt:

> Since persuasion both to truths and falsehoods is urged by means of the art of rhetoric, who would venture to say that truth, in the person of its defenders, ought to stand its ground, unarmed, against falsehood, so that those who are trying to convince us of falsehoods should know how to induce their listeners to be favorably inclined. . . . while the defenders of the truth do not know how to do this? Should the former proclaim their falsehoods briefly, explicitly, and plausibly, while the latter tell the truth in such a way that it is tedious to listen to, difficult to understand, and finally, disagreeable to believe? Should the former, influencing and urging the minds of their listeners to error by their eloquence, terrify, sadden, gladden, and passionately encourage them, while the latter, indifferent and cold in behalf of truth sleep on? Who is so foolish as to claim this?[6]

Isn't it remarkable that he was thinking that way so many centuries ago? For Augustine it was not enough simply to have the truth to proclaim to hearers; a person needed to pay attention to the cultural moment and to find a way right then and there to say it.

So what important cultural phenomenon informs the preacher who needs to preach to a wide intergenerational gathering? To my way of thinking, the phenomenon that affects us all, young and old alike, is the one known as *post-literacy*. Take a minute if you like, and put this chapter down and do a little Web search for *post-literacy*. Actually, the very fact that you knew what I meant by "Web search" and had the capacity to do it is a pretty significant testimony to the claim that we are living in a post-literate culture. With television screens always in view and iPods and cell phones glued to every imaginable ear, who takes time to read or write? This is neither the time nor the place to judge this far-reaching cultural phenomenon. I can only assert that it is so and suggest some implications which those of us called to preach all at once to multiple generations must deal with.

Simply put, post-literate folk are those people who may well be able to read but who, for a laundry list of reasons, choose not to. These are *post-literate* folk, according to theorists like the late Jesuit scholar Walter Ong and the sociologist of religion Tex Sample. They shape their visions, do their ethics, and get through their long days and even longer nights much as their primal ancestors did, in an oral context—by chatting, gossiping, daydreaming, and sympathizing. Sample argues that about *half* of all Americans work "primarily out of a traditional orality." The vast majority of moral and spiritual decision-making data comes to us through television, movies, songs, stories, and conversations—that is to say, tacitly rather than discursively. I am convinced that one reason that sermons seem so distant to people is that they were born in the preacher's mind as a literary phenomenon rather than as an oral one. I am forever writing on students' sermon manuscripts: "[Jack/Jill], this sounds like a term paper, not a sermon—write for the ear and not the eye!" And this is not a matter of mere style either. Traditionally, oral people get at what they need to know not through "discourse, systematic coherence, the consistent use of clear definitions, and the writing of discursive prose," but rather through chatting, gossiping, and daydreaming. Let's look at each of these in turn.

Chatting

Intergenerational preachers will most likely be heard *chatting* their sermons on Sunday morning. By "chatting" I don't mean to trivialize the great work of proclamation—I have given my life to it—but I am trying to suggest that our ears have become conditioned to hear things most comfortably through the uneven rhythms of conversation. There is a reason, after all, why every Starbucks in America devotes so much valuable floor space to tables for four and comfortably stuffed chairs set in pairs. They expect that their clientele will enjoy sipping a latte more while chatting with a friend. Conversation is the way that people hear much of what comes to their ears. Simply consider the enormous proliferation of talk radio and talk TV, which have effectively shaped our ears to hear in a certain way. I know that referring to preaching as "chatting" wrecks our old image of the preacher as the great orator, and to those for whom that is still a treasured image, it will be disappointing; but most people are accustomed to hearing things through the fits and starts of a conversation, and that habit is not likely to be altered just because it is Sunday morning. We can take heart, however, in knowing that the word most used in the New Testament to describe what preachers are doing when they are preaching is a word that simply means *conversation.*[7] In Antioch, where followers of the Way were for the first time called Christians, the renewal movement began with a peculiar kind of preaching as conversation. Acts 11:20 is revealing in this regard: "But among them were some men of Cyprus and Cyrene who, on coming to Antioch, spoke to the Hellenists also, proclaiming the Lord Jesus." The method of their proclamation was conversation, and their good instincts are reason enough for us to follow suit.

There is at least one serious implication of this cultural phenomenon that affects the sermon itself. Sermons prepared and preached with a wide intergenerational gathering in view will most likely be preached without notes and with a pretty loose

relationship to a pulpit or lectern. Notes, manuscripts, and lec-
terns are all signs of a highly literate culture and will have limited
intergenerational appeal. What makes conversations distinctive,
as a rhetorical event, are their spontaneity and responsiveness.
Conversations spring up almost out of nowhere, and when you
find yourself in one, you are never sure where it will end or what
turn it will take. O. Wesley Allen, assistant professor of homiletics at Lexington Theological Seminary, suggests that in conversations, "all participants potentially take on the roles of both
listener and speaker. In give-and-take fashion, all those in a conversation participate in the meaning making of others and invite
others to influence their own meaning making."[8] So, of course,
preaching-as-chatting demands attentiveness on the part of the
preacher. She or he will quite literally have to keep an eye on the
listeners to determine what they need. Here is what Augustine
says about this remarkable dynamic:

> In familiar conversations each one has the opportunity to ask
> questions, but when all are silent to hear one person and are
> looking at him attentively, it is neither customary nor fitting for
> anyone to ask a question about what he does not understand.
> The speaker should be especially watchful, therefore, to assist
> those who are silent. . . . Those who are delivering what they
> have previously prepared and memorized word for word cannot
> do this.[9]

I am taken aback by Augustine's practical sensitivity. And do
remember that this practical advice is coming from the same pen
that gave us *The Confessions* and *The City of God*. One of our
most important theological minds ever is not suggesting that the
theological content of the sermon be "dumbed down" but rather
that it be made more available by the preacher's paying careful attention to the listener.

Gossiping

Look up the word *gossip* in the Oxford English Dictionary, and
you will find all the usual meanings—"a person who chatters" and

"a person who repeats idle talk and rumors." But that dictionary artfully and theologically brings us back to its original meaning, that is, "god-sib," which means "godparent." A gossip is a person who stands with and for the baptized. Isn't that a unique meaning? So maybe that method is what the apostle Paul is up to in so many of his letters when he is constantly commending this sister or that brother. He is gossiping about them in a way to encourage their lives to be lived out in others who observe them. He is speaking on behalf of the baptized, to the baptized, so that all might become what we were always meant to be.

St. Paul knows something about sanctification that we seem to have forgotten a long time ago. Virtue is set in motion in the community of faith not by a wagging finger but by a lived example. Virtue is the product not of "shaming" but of "showing." I encourage my students in preaching to "people their sermons." Obviously this must be done with the permission of those whom they talk about, but I want them to show real examples from real lives of what it means to be a real follower of Jesus Christ. Talking about, gossiping about, the virtues of the beloved in our community turns a kind of spiritual "flywheel" that sets in motion the possibility of virtue.

In his wonderful little book *Open Secrets,* Richard Lischer, professor of preaching at Duke Divinity School, defends the practice of this kind of homiletical gossiping better than anyone I know:

> Gossip is the community's way of conducting moral discourse and, in an oddly indirect way, of forgiving old offenses . . . our gossip was common discourse. It contributed to a moral consensus on, say, what constitutes decent farming, honorable business, tolerable preaching, or effective parenting. Gossip was our community's continuing education.[10]

So let me gossip a bit here and now. My first year in ministry was Art Smallegan's last year on earth. A cancer would rob him of his life one ounce at a time. While his body diminished, his soul expanded. I visited him three or four times a week, mostly for selfish reasons. Every visit was as predictable as a Sunday liturgy—light conversation about life in Hudsonville, the singing of a hymn, the

Blessed Distractions

Howard Vanderwell

Some time ago I visited the Shin-Urayasu Reformed Church in Tokyo, Japan. It's a small congregation that meets in what most of us would consider to be a small worship space. Forty-five straight-back chairs were neatly arranged in rows in this warm, cozy, but compact room.

While the pastor pointed out some of the features of their worship space, two areas caught my attention. First, in one corner of the back, an area was set off, obviously for toddlers. It was a safe place with books and toys, yet it was open to the worship area, so mothers caring for their toddlers could participate in worship.

Then I looked in the other back corner. I saw that four of the straight-back chairs had been turned to face four others in the back row, creating a small platform between them. A small mattress and blanket were placed on that platform.

I pointed to it with a questioning look. "Our infant nursery!" the pastor said proudly.

I smiled, and then I asked, "Does the noise ever bother you when you are leading worship?"

His face lit up, and his eyes sparkled as he answered, "Oh, no! They are our children!"

reading of a passage from the Bible, and then finally a prayer for grace. One day, near the end of the summer, with Art's strength and life about to leave him, my nervousness and pastoral inexperience made a shambles of the liturgy.

I entered Art's bedroom with death hanging on the curtains. Geraldine, Art's wife of 50-plus years, was sitting on the end of the bed quietly weeping. Art was hidden beneath what appeared to me to be a coma. There would be no light conversation about life in Hudsonville this day. I was too frightened to sing a hymn, and the combination of Geraldine's weeping and Art's coma excluded the usual Bible reading. I knelt at the side of Art's bed and began to pray. I prayed for Art and Geraldine, for their children and grand-children, and I prayed for our congregation. Finishing my prayer, I quietly whispered "Amen" and got up to leave. At that moment Art summoned the strength to make what would be among his last moves. He reached out with his long, tawny Dutch fingers and grabbed my necktie. Pulling me to within a few inches of his face, he whispered, "Don't forget to read the Bible?" I fumbled over myself to find my little pocket Bible to correct my colossal pastoral blunder. And I read.

Doesn't Art's story make you want to read your Bible tonight? That is the point of gossiping.

Daydreaming

While exiled on the island of Patmos, and left to vultures, St. John was given an extraordinary vision that sustained him—and count-less millions ever since. A voice like the sound of a trumpet com-pelled him: "Come up here and I will show you what must take place after this" (Rev. 4:1). In that moment John, like so many oth-ers before him, was given a sustaining vision; and we who are called to preach to multiple generations at one time are given a peculiar practice that I call daydreaming. Daydreaming is the practicing of envisioning within the sermon a better future for everyone based on gospel truth. It is a peculiar kind of speech that is imaginative but not fictitious, hopeful but not maudlin, compelling but still resistible. This argument is artfully made by Walter Brueggeman in his compelling book *Finally Comes The Poet: Daring Speech for Proclamation*. I'll let him speak for himself:

> The issues facing the church and its preachers may be put this way: Is there another way to speak? Is there another voice to be voiced? Is there an alternative universe of discourse to be practiced that will struggle with the truth in ways unreduced? In the sermon—and in the life of the church, more generally, I propose—we are to practice another way of communication that makes another shaping of life possible: unembarrassed about rationality, not anxious about accommodating the rea-son of the age.

The task and possibility of preaching is to open out the good news of the gospel with alternative modes of speech—speech that is dramatic, artistic, and capable of inviting persons to join in another conversation. . . . The church on Sunday morning, or whenever it engages in its odd speech, may be the last place left in our society for imaginative speech that permits people to enter into new worlds of faith and to participate in joyous, obedient life.[11]

There is a scene in a stage adaptation of L. Frank Baum's *The Wizard of Oz*[12] that I think you will enjoy and that helps me express what I mean by daydreaming in a sermon. In this scene Dorothy comes home from school later than she should have and catches the wrath of Auntie Em. As you listen to their exchanges, keep in the back of your mind our need to develop more effective ways to help people see new gospel worlds rising up out of our fall-framed existences. *"Come up here and I will show you what must take place after this!"* Now Dorothy and Auntie Em in a struggle between two worlds:

> "In wadin' were you, Missy?"
>
> "No. I jus' like to sit on the bank an' look inside!" says Dorothy with a girlish excitement.
>
> "Inside o' what?," responds Auntie Em.
>
> "The crick."
>
> "A crick ain't got insides . . . it's on'y got a bottom. An' there ain't nothin' to see—on'y stones an' fish swimmin' around," says Auntie Em *[sounding to me like a realist without a pulse]*.
>
> "Is that all you see in a crick, Aunt Em?" Dorothy responds *[suggesting that she has a gospel world of daydreaming]*.
>
> "It's all any Christian can see, Dorothy. . . ."
>
> "[Auntie Em], didn't you ever look quick at a fish an' think first off it was a mermaid maybe?" *[Be careful, Dorothy—this is the demythologized 20th century.]*
>
> "Dor'thy!"
>
> "I have lotso' times, Auntie Em!"
>
> "That ain't right, Dor'thy!"
>
> "Why?" pleads Dorothy.

"If the good Lord had wanted us to see mermaids swimmin'
through our cow pasture he'd o' put 'em there Himself. . . .
[But didn't you ever pretend things, Aunt Em?]

Auntie Em's view of things is opaque; she seems incapable of
daydreaming. Dorothy's view of things is transparent. She has responded to the invitation *"Come up here and I will show you what
must take place after this!"* To borrow a Kennedyesque construc-
tion from the 1960s, really to lean on the school of the prophet
and the evangelist, Auntie Em sees what is and wonders "Why?"
Dorothy sees what ought to be and wonders, "Why not?"

And daydreams have sustained the brightest and best for a
long, long time. Here's a short list of some of my most honored
daydreamers from our recent memory . . .

Do you know the name of Phoebe Palmer? She pumped revival
into the boroughs of New York at the turn of the 19th century
with a Bible in one hand and a soupspoon in the other. She was a
daydreamer, and I want to preach in a way that would sustain her
dreams.

How about Dietrich Bonhoeffer? He did not consider academic privilege a thing to be grasped but emptied himself (like
somebody else we know), until he was hung out to dry in the
howling winds of Nazi hatred (like somebody else we know). He
was a daydreamer, and I want to preach in a way that would sustain his dreams.

How about Dorothy Day? A daughter of wealth and privilege
who gave up the life of the swirling cocktail-party debutante to
pick up the life of towel and basin? Her passion started the Catholic Worker movement that has meant much to so many. She was a
daydreamer, and I want to preach in a way that would sustain her
dreams.

And there are more daydreamers than these: How about Sim-
one Weil? Millard Fuller? Mother Teresa? And listen to me—am I
forgetting the biggest daydreamer of our time? In a single afternoon,
with a wild-eyed daydream, Martin Luther King, Jr., reshaped our
social consciousness and made it impossible to live easy in the land
with racial hatred in your heart. They were daydreamers one and
all, and I want to preach in a way that will sustain their dreams.

Back to Our Question

So let me get this straight: you expect me to preach a sermon for 20 minutes that will inform, persuade, and delight everyone from an 80-year-old with a hearing problem to an eight-year-old *with a hearing problem*. Yes, this is precisely what all the gathered faithful expect the preachers to do. It will not be easy, but it's simple; with a little more focus on the Word (the process of discovering what we are to learn), and a little more focus on the listener (the process of presenting what we have learned), we can do it!

Discussion Questions

1. Describe the characteristics of some of the best intergenerational communicators you have ever heard.

2. Have you ever had an experience like the one I described listening to the Gospel of Mark? How did it make you feel?

3. What would it take for you to memorize longer portions of Scripture and to share them publicly?

4. One of the practices that I didn't discuss is the implementation of preaching teams, including a wider intergenerational range of communicators from Sunday to Sunday. Who could join in the preaching of the Word in your congregational context?

5. Gossip a little with one another about some of the noble saints who have made a difference in your life.

Timothy Brown has been a pastor of two thriving congregations and knows the challenge and adventure of presenting sermons to congregations on a weekly basis. Currently he serves as the Henry Bast professor of preaching at Western Theological Seminary in Holland, Michigan.

CHAPTER 8

One Congregation's Story

Stan Mast

Perhaps one of the most frequently asked questions in congregations is this: "But won't we have to change our whole worship style if we are going to keep the generations together?" One large city church tackled that question directly, did the research, and sought to answer the questions helpfully. Its desire to ask hard questions about the effectiveness of ministry to youth and young adults in the context of such a worship style led members to undertake a yearlong study about the relationship of youth to the style of worship. This study was sponsored and funded by the Calvin Institute of Christian Worship. Stan Mast is one of the pastors of that congregation, and he is in a position to explain the answer the researchers found and what led them to their conclusions.

Is it possible to keep all ages actively engaged in the life of the church and passionately involved in its worship if that church has a formal, traditional, liturgical style of worship? Or are those correct who claim that the worship life of the church must be completely changed, particularly if we hope to keep our youth engaged?

That was the question at the center of a yearlong study conducted by the church where I am the pastor, the LaGrave Avenue Christian Reformed Church in Grand Rapids, Michigan.

A Traditional Intergenerational Church

Our congregation is a historic (120-year-old) tall-steeple church in downtown Grand Rapids, at the edge of the business community and a block from the Heartside District, where the poorest of the poor live in our city. Over the past 15 or so years, our membership has increased 50 percent to over 1500, with hundreds of new members of all ages. A study of our community would show almost equal-sized slices of generations, with slightly more members in the very young and very old groups and slightly fewer in the family-with-teenagers category. The membership profile of our congregation indicates that 25 percent of our members are 25 years old or younger, 17 percent are between 25 and 40, 28 percent are between 41 and 65, and 29 percent are 65 or older. LaGrave Church has long been marked by traditional worship, and nearly all of those who have come in the last 15 years were drawn by that worship. In other words, LaGrave is a fully intergenerational church with a deep historical commitment to traditional worship.

Our study of youth and worship was shaped by the LaGrave Vision Statement: "LaGrave CRC will strive to be a Worshiping Community committed to maintaining a tradition of formal worship which integrates articulate and intelligent preaching of God's Word with music that glorifies God and inspires worshipers. . . ." A newly adopted five-year strategic plan included the following goals:

- LaGrave will develop and implement ways by which its tradition of formal worship will be inspirational and understandable to our members, including children and young people, and to our visitors.
- While we do not plan to alter our tradition of formal worship, LaGrave will investigate and implement ways in which participation in worship can be made increasingly accessible to our children and youth.

These goals drove our study of worship and youth. Concern for youth in worship has always been integral to the life of La-Grave Church. Our Dutch immigrant church was the first in our denomination to use English in worship, and the reason for that scandalous innovation was concern for the youth. In his wonderful book prepared for LaGrave's centennial celebration, *A Century of Grace,* emeritus minister Jacob Eppinga reports that four motives drove the formation of this first English-speaking congregation in the CRC:

> first, to provide our young people with the means of grace in a language they could understand; second, to keep them in our denomination, that its growth may not be retarded, its best life blood transferred into other ecclesiastical bodies; third, that in generations to come we may preserve the old Reformed principles of our fathers, though clothed in the dress of a new language; and fourth, to remove the language barriers that we might be able to spread our Calvinistic principles in ever-widening circles and thus carry out God's great purpose in bringing our ancestors to these shores.[1]

So this study of youth and worship was entirely in keeping with the pioneering spirit of our founding fathers and mothers.

A Nervous Church

As every reader of this book knows all too well, any tinkering with worship is a hot-button issue. We were no different. Some members of the older generation were afraid that this was the beginning of the end of traditional worship. Despite constant reassurances to the contrary, they were anxious. How could they not be? A number of them had come from churches where a bit of experimentation with "youth worship" had led to what they viewed as a wholesale rejection of traditional worship in favor of a more informal contemporary style. Their own history made them cautious toward the dangers of what they saw as "fiddling" with worship.

Besides, changes occurring across nearly the whole church landscape in America (at least as portrayed in the popular press) supported their fears. To attract and keep young people, thousands of churches have adopted what they think is youth-friendly contemporary worship. And for a decade or more, many voices have loudly proclaimed, "That's the only way it can be done."

On the other end of the generational spectrum, some of our youth and their leaders were afraid that our study could never find ways to incorporate teenagers fully in the worship life of the congregation, that nothing would change after our study. "Even if we do find ways to 'tweak' our worship, the older generation will never allow these changes," they said.

However, we think we have discovered or rediscovered some considerations that should be helpful to any church committed both to a particular style of worship (whether traditional or contemporary, vintage or "seeker") and to the younger generations as well as the older. The discriminating reader will want to know upfront how we made these discoveries. As any scientist will attest, if the research process is flawed, the results can't be trusted.

A Difficult Process

Our investigation began with reading and discussing eight books on subjects related to youth and worship.[2] We engaged in direct discussions with our church's youth and their parents. With guidance from the Calvin Institute of Christian Worship, we consulted with a number of experts on youth and worship and invited some of those experts to speak to our congregation in our adult education hour.[3] Finally, we visited a number of churches that reputedly were already doing what we were striving to do.

It must be said that we had a difficult time finding such churches. Following every lead we were given, we virtually scoured the country looking for churches with traditional worship that were doing an effective job of involving youth in the ways specified in our mandate. We did find a few such churches, and they were helpful. However, many of the traditional churches told us directly that they are not doing a good job of including teens in worship. With very few teens attending their traditional worship services, they minister to the teens by developing large and dynamic youth programs and by offering alternative youth-oriented worship services. Other reportedly traditional churches were no longer traditional in style, having decided that the only way to minister to youth was to allow youth culture to totally shape their worship. Indeed, one megachurch youth leader flatly told our visiting team that what we were trying to do "simply can't be done. You have to bring youth culture into the church. That's the only way to reach them."

Indeed, most of the churches we studied (both traditional and contemporary) had a very small percentage of their teens attending their worship services. There simply was no intergenerational worship happening in the churches that we thought we could consider as models. In their admirable and passionate efforts to reach teens in worship by changing worship style, they have given up on intergenerational traditional worship as an idea whose time has passed. We were discouraged by these visits.

Even these disappointing visits, however, helped us form some helpful conclusions for intergenerational worship in our traditional church. We discovered that at least five elements must work together if a church is going to minister to youth effectively. The first two have to do specifically with worship, the last three with other dimensions of the church's life that may be even more important than the worship.

A Passion for God

From a number of sources, we have learned that it isn't really style that captures the minds and hearts of teens; it is passion. Contemporary wisdom assumes that teens are turned off by traditional worship because of the music. However, according to our research, that assumption is not true. Although teens are obviously passionate about their music, we discovered that it is possible to provide passionate worship without adopting music from youth culture.

When we interviewed LaGrave teens and their parents about what they were looking for in worship, we heard a wide variety of responses. In general, our teens were not asking LaGrave to adopt a worship style or music style aimed primarily at them, though they did suggest a greater variety in instruments, anthems, and style of hymns. Some even said that, although they love "their" music outside of church, it simply doesn't "sound right" in church. Some of their friends who were not members disagreed. But music was not the focus of such comments. In fact, the most surprising response from our own teens was their emphasis on preaching.

The Church at Prayer

Randy Engle

North Hills Church has a bookmark in every Bible in its sanctuary. On each bookmark is the name of a child of the congregation, with the verse "I have no greater joy than to hear that my children are walking in the truth" (1 John 3:4). Periodic bulletin announcements remind worshipers to pray for the child whose name is on their bookmark. But as with a lot of good ideas, enthusiasm dries up over time. The bookmarks were almost pulled from the Bibles. That is, until one memorable children's sermon.

The children's sermon leader pulled the bookmarks out of the Bibles. When the children came forward, she explained how important it is that we pray for each other. Then she said, "Rather than just talk about that today, we're going to *do* it! And because you are so important to this church, here's how we'll do it." She asked each child to take a bookmark to someone in the sanctuary. Each person was asked to pray for the child whose name was on the bookmark. However, the children were given permission to keep their eyes open and watch as the church prayed for them.

The layers of theological beauty here are probably incalculable. But the one I shall never forget is the awe of so many children—grown-up children included—watching the church *be* church.

That is, their most frequent comment about worship had to do not with worship style or musical offerings, but with sermons and preaching style. (See the section below, "An Active Participant," for more on this topic.)

One of our consultants, Jane Vann, a Presbyterian elder and professor of Christian education, was most helpful on this subject of passion. What teens really object to, she said, is "going through the motions." It isn't so much traditional worship that leaves teens cold; it is "conventional" worship, predictable worship in which people seem to be participating only by rote and empty habit. Teens are looking for passion. In a memorable slogan, she advised, "Youth are heat-seeking missiles; they will go where there is fire."[4] Her identification of this concern helped us focus on three considerations.

God-centered

How one defines passion will vary from person to person, but three things seem to be central to passionate worship. First, the service must focus on God—not on fun or form, not on excitement or excellence, not even on being edified by the service, but on giving praise and glory to the triune God. Or as Vann summarized it, "Worship must be relaxed joyful reverence."

Psalm 95 helps to explain that unusual definition of worship. At the heart of passionate worship is *reverence* for God. "O Come, let us worship and bow down, let us kneel before the Lord, our Maker!" (verse 6). The fundamental posture of worship is kneeling or, better, stretching out full-length on the ground before God, not out of abject fear but in loving adoration of God's goodness. "For he is our God and we are the people of his pasture" (verse 7). Such reverence expresses itself mainly in a willingness to listen carefully to God; that is, the main way we show reverence is to close our mouths, open our ears, soften our hearts, and do what God tells us to do.

But passionate worship is not only reverence; it is also *joyful* reverence. "[L]et us make a joyful noise to the rock of our salvation! . . . let us make a joyful noise to him with songs of praise! For the Lord is a great God" (verses 1–3). Interestingly, joy comes not only from realizing that God is good, but also from celebrating that God is great. We rejoice that "Our God is an awesome God," because God's greatness is expressed in mighty acts on our behalf.

Passionate God-centered worship is *relaxed* joyful reverence—not lazy or sloppy or casual or flippant. It can't be any of those things because reverence is at the heart of worship. But worship can be *relaxed* because when we worship, we rest in Christ. It's not first of all about *us*—about our performance, our excellence, our offerings of praise. It's all about Jesus and what he has already done for us. When we rest in his finished work, we can relax in God's presence as children loved beyond measure. Worship becomes passionate when we understand grace. It is the death and resurrection of Jesus that makes us pleasing to God. We can rest in his work and offer back to God the passionate worship that is relaxed joyful reverence.

Spiritually Formative

Second, we learned that this focus on God in worship must grow out of the entire church's focus on spiritual formation. If the whole congregation is conscious of its need to be formed in the image of Christ, if people are growing in their intimate walk with Christ, this will make corporate worship a passionate event. If the individual members of a church aren't walking closely with Christ, it will be nearly impossible for corporate worship to be filled with a passion for God. Worship leaders can whip themselves into a frenzy of preparation and performance and even prayer (remember the prophets of Baal on Mount Carmel), but if the congregation has not entered into worship after spending the week in close communion with God, the members will not worship passionately.

Effective Leadership

Third, it is crucial that the leaders up front be spiritually "into" the worship. This means much more than spending moments or even hours in prayer before a service. The leaders must be passionate about Christ in their daily lives, engaging in spiritual disciplines that will be used by the Spirit to shape them more and more in the image of Christ. Then, spiritual preparation specifically for worship will enable them to be channels of grace and truth. In other words, effective worship leadership must arise out of an entire life that is marked by spiritual health and vitality.

An Active Participant

If we want teens to be passionate in their worship, we must give them opportunities to participate in that worship. There are a number of ways they can be involved: in preparation, in the pews, up front, and in reflection afterward.

In Preparation

Teens can help plan worship services, whether as regular members of a worship committee, as members of ad hoc groups that help the pastors and musicians plan the services for a liturgical season (or other time span), or as a small group that suggests preaching subjects to the pastor. As we became more aware of the importance of youth participation, I met with our youth group to ask for subjects I could preach on during the upcoming year of intergenerational worship. For an hour the youth peppered me with a wide variety of ideas. Some of the ideas were related to their personal lives (predictable peer pressure, painful eating disorders, personal body image, and self-doubt); others talked about theological questions (heaven, universalism, unanswered prayers, and disappointment with God); and still others focused on larger social issues (child abuse, gambling, stem-cell research). In the end, I had 25 meaty subjects to focus on next year. Then I gathered a group of eight teenage volunteers to help me plan the services and sermons for the fall section of our year of focus on intergenerational worship. I asked them such questions as: What thoughts come to mind when you hear that I'm going to address this particular subject in a sermon? Can you think of any songs, movies, or experiences that illustrate this subject? Would you like to participate in the service itself? In the end they planned an entire service focused on "The Unbalanced Family," emphasizing their desire for more time with their parents. All of this preparatory work behind the scenes resulted in services of passionate worship and sermons much better than average.

In the Pew

We can also help youth participate in worship by involving them in the pew. And that requires some careful worship planning, so that they can participate from the heart. While not calling for a wholesale change in our worship style, both our youth and our consultants told us that teens must be able to relate to the music if they are to give praise and glory from their hearts. Thus, we worked hard at using a variety of music throughout the intergenerational year, while still maintaining our formal, liturgical style. These services included some popular "youth" choruses, some choir anthems with a youth theme, and frequent participation of teens in playing instruments or singing.

Equally important was the use of language in worship that communicated with youth—not slang or "street language" but just clear, ordinary, visual language. Further, for youth to be involved, the liturgy must call for some response on their part. That is, the liturgy can't be merely elevated and beautiful; it must call for a real response from all ages. Perhaps that response may be a greater commitment to obedience, a deeper spirit of gratitude, and new efforts at healthier relationships.

The Oldest and the Youngest

Carol Rottman

Jack and Abel were both pushed up a ramp into the church—one in a wheelchair and the other in a stroller. Jack came to celebrate his 100th birthday; Abel came to embrace God's covenant promises, as a child of believers. Jack Koorndyk came early to savor the day and to greet old friends. Abel den Dulk's family got there just in time, after getting four children presentable for their moments around the baptismal font.

During the service, Jack recalled stories of his own baptism at Eastern Avenue Church, in this very building, 100 years earlier. As he glanced around the sanctuary, he could almost see his bride, Minnie, coming down the aisle. He could almost feel the

Finally, as elaborated above, the sermons and prayers must clearly and specifically address the concerns of youth, as well as those of other age groups. Our task force on youth and worship was surprised that youth were more concerned about preaching than about worship style or music. They want to "get something out of it." And it's not enough that the sermons are generally relevant, that they raise common human concerns or widely discussed world problems. While not every sermon has to be on a subject that targets the concerns of youth, the youth must be specifically hooked into the sermon with a story or a reference to youth culture or a uniquely youth-oriented issue. They told us that they don't even hear the sermon, no matter how good it might be, if they aren't pulled out of their Sunday-morning reverie by something "youthful" in the sermon.

Up Front

There is a whole variety of ways in which teens can participate up front. Acts as simple as ushering or leading the procession are ways they can contribute to the worship of God's people. Perhaps riskier—but a step eagerly embraced by many young people—we

water of baptism on the heads of his two children. As Pastor Thea Leunk preached, Jack remembered the string of preachers who had catechized and led him in faith over the years, while challenging modernism, heresy, and sometimes the church order.

After the service, Jack enjoyed a piece of his birthday cake among a party of hundreds. Abel preferred milk from a bottle. Their family of believers gathered around to celebrate God's faithfulness over the generations.

Abel will not remember this day, except for the photograph of himself, dressed in a white baptismal gown and cradled in the loving arms of Jack Koorndyk—the day when the oldest and youngest members of one particular church, within the great church universal, joined briefly on a rare and wonder-filled day of grace.

had them reading the Scripture lessons for the day, leading the congregational prayer, playing instruments, or singing. In fact, the traditional churches we visited that have the most dynamic inter-generational worship were involving all ages in a whole succession of graded choirs led by skilled and charismatic leaders.

On occasions young people have given testimonies about how mission trips or other experiences have changed their lives. Liturgical dance has given some young people an opportunity to show their love for God by physical movement. All of these participatory acts can take place in any kind of worship style and have been warmly embraced by our intergenerational congregation. In fact, we try hard to use the generations together in as many of these activities as possible; for example, having the three generations of a family light the candles in the Advent wreath, or asking a mother and son to lead the confession.

Afterward

Finally, teens can become more involved in traditional worship if their feedback to the sermon or service is elicited in discussions with the pastor or other worship leader. It can be healthy for worship leaders to engage youth in sessions to evaluate specific services. Discussing with them what helped them pray, engage with God, and relate to other worshipers can be helpful for all. And classes explaining the how and the why of worship may be helpful in stimulating participation. No one enjoys doing something he or she doesn't understand or do well.

A Welcoming Place

Teens must feel that the church is *their* place, a place where they truly belong. We heard from a number of our consultants that this is perhaps the most important dimension in keeping teens engaged in traditional worship. In fact, we heard them say that it doesn't matter what a church does *in* worship, if a young person doesn't feel at home in the church *before* and *after* worship. Before a church can involve its teens in worship of any style, that church must accept, value, love, and involve those teens in the overall life of the church. If teens feel they are valued and loved members of the entire church community, they will almost automatically feel part of the worship experience.

Being loved and valued means that people notice them, know them by name, are interested in their lives, and accept them even when they act in ways that might be objectionable. One of our senior members, upon hearing these findings, made it a point to learn the names of 10 teens in the next several months. With pen and paper in hand, he introduced himself to teens in the hallways of church and wrote down their names. He discovered that teens are a bit taken aback by this direct approach, but the idea is on the mark. We have assigned every teen a prayer partner who maintains light but constant contact with that young person throughout the year. Intergenerational mission trips to Honduras have put three generations at work on erecting a house. The community that resulted made the teens and the seniors feel part of something larger and more important than their own lives. Finally, it is especially important that the pastors lead the charge in making teens feel loved. Simply knowing their names is an important step, and actually talking with them about the state of their lives pays huge dividends, even if it is only a conversation about the game or the concert.

A Parental Commitment

If a church is going to involve teens, the help of their parents is essential. To help young people understand and appreciate worship, parents must also be passionate worshipers. If parents are critical or prefer a different style of worship, it is unlikely that a church can make its worship attractive to the teens of that family. In fact, we have discovered that in some families the dissatisfaction of the youth was driven by the unhappiness of their boomer parents. When parents carry their own youthful negative reactions to traditional worship into their 40s and 50s, it does not help their children to embrace the worship of their church. It is essential that parents are loyal to the worship of their church, whatever its worship style.

Loyalty to worship means at the very least that the parents regularly attend worship themselves and bring their youth along with them. Often this is not the case. This "bringing" should begin in early childhood, when children are most open to the influence of their parents and to "soaking up" the world around them. One of our consultants, Ed Seely, a longtime church educator and youth specialist, said, "Humanly speaking, the key to keeping young people in the faith is at home in early childhood."[5] But, adds another consultant, Carol Lytch, then the coordinator of Lilly Endowment programs at Louisville Presbyterian Seminary, it is also important that parents

> [maintain] the church attendance rule even into the teen years. Since it is no longer possible to coerce teens to attend church by the time they are high school seniors, parents must persuade teens of the value of the "rule" about church attendance. They do this by setting an example of attending church, by fostering a warm family climate and a thick, religion-infused culture in the home, and by maximizing other family factors.[6]

Parents can help their youth appreciate worship by teaching them what is happening in worship and then discussing services and sermons so that teens get the opportunity to reflect on what just happened in worship. For example, Carolyn Brown, another Christian educator, encourages parents to spend the time on the way home from church talking with their children about "take-aways." (What did you take away from that worship service? How did you experience God's presence there? What helped you to worship this morning?) This "action and reflection" dynamic will help teens get involved spiritually and intellectually in worship.[7]

Finally, we discovered that many parents may need help in this whole area. What do you do when your young person refuses to attend church? How do you lead meaningful devotions? How can you share your own faith in a way that encourages the faith of your children? What will make your family life warm and enjoyable? Some of our teens said that they would love to spend a night at home with their parents just playing games, but that everyone

Blending a Bible Study Group

Cathy Robbs Turner

The Lessons for Life Sunday school class at Christ United Methodist Church has from 12 to 15 members from different generations present each week. We have children and their parents, singles, widows, and married couples, of various ages. Initially, class members ranged in age from Leasa at 35 to Ray at 70. Then we added John and his lovely young daughter, Amy, who did not know anyone in the middle-school class and just wanted to be with her dad. We adopted her and found that she added a great deal to discussion with her youthful perspective. Then Robyn came and brought Chelsia, who is 17, and her little brother, Brandon, who is 10. Before you knew it, we had several children joining us at one time or another.

We love the blending of the generations as we study the Bible and discuss relevant current events. We get many diverse insights from our members, who now range in age from 8 to 80. Our collection just happened, but we all are blessed by the presence of the young and old together. The varied backgrounds and ages of the members contribute to fellowship and learning. Our class is a great prelude to worship.

is too busy. How can we deal with this situation? And speaking specifically about worship, it may be necessary to offer classes on worship to parents so that they can explain worship to their children.

A Dynamic Program

We heard from our consultants and parents that a real key to keeping teens in churches is a dynamic youth group and high-quality educational programs for youth. Even if teens aren't all that fond of a church's style of worship, great programs will help keep them in the church. A youth program that focuses on actually discipling young people instead of merely providing them with an array of enjoyable activities is essential. While play is important, prayer and Bible study and worship in a more youth-friendly format will build the kind of fully devoted disciples of Jesus Christ who will want to engage in passionate worship, no matter what its style. And we heard from the parents of our teens that if they like their church-school class, if that class engages them in a meaningful educational experience, those youth do not complain about the worship. But if they are already bored or turned off by educational programs before or after worship, they will not be eager to return to church at all.

Picking up an earlier theme in this chapter, we heard again and again that it is absolutely essential for parents to support the church's programs for youth and to insist that their youth attend. The church may have excellent programs, but if teens don't participate in them, they simply won't be tied in to their church. Parents are crucial to the involvement of their teens.

Summary

If a church wants to have genuinely intergenerational worship, it should not think first of all and automatically of a change in worship or musical style, but about the five p's—*passion, participation, place, parents,* and *programs.* First, a church can involve all the generations in worship by developing a churchwide mindset that places a passion for God at the center of worship. Every church must find ways to help all ages realize that worship is not first of all about "getting something" out of worship, but about "giving something" to God in worship—namely, the praise and glory that are God's due.

Second, a church that seeks to be intergenerational in worship must find creative ways to help its youth participate actively in worship services. Youth can help to plan occasional services and provide responsible feedback after services. They can lead worship as readers, singers, leaders of prayer, liturgical dancers, and so forth. Further, to encourage young people to be passionate in their worship, worship must employ a variety of music that fits into the basic style and language that communicates to youth, addressing their concerns (as well those of adults) in sermons and prayers.

Third, a church must adopt strategies that will strengthen relationships between all the generations throughout the church, so that all will experience church as a welcoming place. Every child and teen must know that he or she is a treasured member of the congregation, and relationships between teens and nonparental adults are central to that aim.

Fourth, creating intergenerational worship depends heavily on the support and involvement of parents. Thus, a church must help parents in their task of encouraging the full participation of their children in the life of the church. There may be a need to provide specific instruction about worship to parents as well as to young people, so that they will understand and appreciate worship. These efforts will also include encouraging parents to provide the kind of religious life at home that is conducive to their children's spiritual growth.

Fifth, to capture the allegiance of youth, an intergenerational church must find ways to get them involved in the youth and educational programs of the church. In addition to creating the best programs possible, this may also mean involving youth as leaders, helpers, and mentors in the children's programs.

Our study convinced us that efforts to make traditional and liturgical worship engaging for all generations is possible, and well worth it.

Discussion Questions

1. What is your overall reaction to the premise of this chapter? What are its strengths? Its weaknesses?

2. In what specific ways can your church foster God-centered worship?

3. How realistic for your church is the section on participation?

4. In what creative ways can your church help generations feel at home?

5. What can a church do if parents are not supportive of the church and its worship?

Stan Mast is the minister of preaching at LaGrave Avenue Christian Reformed Church in Grand Rapids, Michigan. The LaGrave Avenue Church is a large, historic church in the downtown area of the city with formal and liturgical worship.

CHAPTER 9

Intergenerational Connectors in Worship

Laura and Robert J. Keeley

The authors are a husband-and-wife team who work together as worship planners for their congregation. They have written curriculum materials for children and youth. In this chapter they draw on their experience and insight to shine the spotlight on many locations in the life of a congregation where the multiple generations can become and remain connected.

An intergenerational congregation is easy to imagine. As families grow and have children and grandchildren, it is natural that our churches would be filled with people of many generations. Yet without some sort of intervention, worship services can often be strictly by adults, for adults. As we plan worship, it is easy to forget to incorporate children, teens, and the senior adults into the natural ebb and flow of worship. In this chapter we look at practical ways to connect the generations in worship. We are not thinking here about special services that feature a particular age group. Youth services, for example, can reinforce the notion that the other 51 weeks of worship are not for them. Instead, we hope that participation by children, young people, and adults of all ages can become a natural part of the weekly life of the worshiping community, so that the way we worship reflects who we are.

Preparing for Worship

The places where we gather to worship are important. Some congregations have spaces designed specifically for worship, while others meet in places used for other purposes during the week and transformed into worship spaces on Sunday mornings. In either case, the work of preparing the space for worship can be elaborate, or as simple as displaying flowers. Including teens and children in this task uses their gifts, builds community, and provides an opportunity for adult members of the congregation to mentor them. One church in our area schedules a Saturday work morning to decorate the church for Advent. This activity has become a multigenerational event that includes doughnuts, juice, and coffee. Working together hanging wreaths and lights gives young and old members a chance for involvement in a service project that requires a minimal time commitment but makes a difference in the church's life.

The seasons of the church year are often reflected in the colors of the paraments that adorn the communion table and pulpit. By asking children to change these hangings during the worship service, one congregation increased its awareness of the changing seasons. The Christmas Eve service, for example, ended with a song during which a team of children, accompanied by two adults, came forward and replaced the purple Advent colors with the white linens of Christmas so that the sanctuary was prepared for Christmas morning. On Easter morning a team of children again replaced the purple linens of Lent with white for Easter. This time they even changed the pastor's stole. The congregation saw the pastor come down from the pulpit and lower his head so that the child, standing on a step, could replace his purple Lenten stole with a white one. In other congregations, the worship space is stripped on Maundy Thursday.

For years, in churches of some Christian traditions, children have served as acolytes, lighting candles before worship. Our friend Marv is pastor of a church that lights a Christ candle at the front of the sanctuary every week. Worship planners, recognizing that the lighting of this candle before worship was a good way to include children, asked the third-graders to take turns lighting the candle. This practice soon evolved into a ritual that takes place during the opening song: two third-graders walk down the center aisle, one with the light and one carrying the Bible for the pulpit. The children light the candle and bring the Word of God into the sanctuary; at the end of the service, they take the Word and the Light out, symbolizing that this congregation carries God's message to the world as it leaves worship. The children wear stoles, which vary in color as the church year progresses, and they take their jobs seriously. Occasionally the candle in the sanctuary is too tall for a third-grader to reach. The pastor or another adult helps the child light the candle. These images of the pastor and children together preparing the space for worship remind the congregation that worship is for all of God's people. The congregation sometimes sees the kids with their stoles, the light, and the Bible—but also with the orange sneakers they wore to church that morning. As they carry the light out of the sanctuary, the last two steps are often a little hurried as they rush to see which one can blow out the candle.

Many congregations give worshipers the opportunity to spend time with the Bible passage that will be the sermon text for the following Sunday. Some simply print the passage in the bulletin the week before it is to be used, but that practice may be insufficient to encourage people to read the Scripture. Sending the Bible texts to the members by e-mail early in the week might better invite worshipers to engage this part of Scripture. Adding questions that families can discuss may help children and teens come to the service ready to listen to the sermon; and a special invitation targeted to youngsters will make clear that everyone, not only adults, can prepare for worship.

Invitations to participate should also be warmly extended to another group that sometimes feels left out of the mainstream life of the church—single adults. A friend of ours moved to a new community soon after graduation from college to begin teaching. She started attending a local church, and one family made a point of welcoming her not only into the church but also into their pew and into their home. She always knew she had someone to sit with for worship, and this consistent act of hospitality made her more quickly feel a part of the congregation and enabled her to get to know the children of this family and, through them, other children of the church. This simple act of ministry on the part of one family had ripples throughout the life of this young woman and the congregation. Young single adults are not the only singles in a congregation. Older adults who either have long been single or, through life circumstances, are recently single are just as appreciative of hospitality.

Music as a Connector, Not a Divider

Music is, of course, an important part of worship. Because of the way music can speak to the hearts of people of all ages, we need to make sure that we use the music of many generations in our worship. Disagreements over the style of worship often turn out to be mostly disagreements over musical styles. Although these disputes sometimes arise along generational lines, it is not always the case that older members fall on one side of the argument and younger members on the other. Children can and should learn to sing many of the great hymns of the church. Likewise, adults can share in the joy of singing well-constructed children's songs or contemporary hymns that have rich texts and are introduced in a way that fits with the rest of the worship service.

But you don't need to discard your congregation's accustomed style of music to be intergenerational. With a little thought and planning, music of many styles and from many parts of the world can speak to all members. For instance, have the children rehearse and sing the first verse of a familiar hymn, and invite the congregation to join for the other verses. This practice allows children to have a place in leadership while helping them learn a song that has been meaningful to the church for generations.

Many ages of people can participate in groups of vocalists or instrumentalists to support the singing. Brass groups, an orchestra, rhythm instruments, choirs, and praise bands can use members of various ages. Children can play an offertory or prelude. A talented beginner can play at least the melody of a familiar hymn. Adding an adult to play a duet with this young person can help keep a steady tempo and offer another opportunity for mentoring. Such a

Singing the Catechism

Bruce Benedict

Our congregation is young, with many families from a predominantly non-Reformed background. Few of them know the Westminster Shorter Catechism. So we looked for a method by which we could familiarize them with the catechism.

However, instead of teaching a traditional recitation of the catechism, we teach it to the children by singing it. We have set the whole Shorter Catechism to music. We take from 10 to 15 minutes each Sunday morning before regular Sunday school to learn a new question every few weeks. Our leader sings the question and the children respond by singing the answer. When they have polished off a number of questions, they sing them in worship to support sermons or seasonal themes.

A highlight of this year took place on Easter Sunday when they sang Question 38 of the Catechism this way:

Leader: What benefits do believers receive from Christ as the resurrection?
Choir: *At the resurrection, believers, being raised up in glory, shall be openly acknowledged and acquitted in the day of judgment, and made perfectly blessed in the full enjoying of God to all eternity.*

It was a strange and beautiful liturgical experience!

Each family with younger children in our congregation receives a Shorter Catechism CD as a tangible means of supporting the family's engagement in the process of filling their children's hearts with biblical truth.

musical offering can be effective at certain times in the service—as a response to the sermon, for example, or after the prayer of confession. Children or teens who are good singers can be used along with adults as soloists or in small ensembles to introduce new music to the congregation. Music does not need to be elaborate to be effective; and simple parts, done with proper rehearsal and preparation, can allow children to participate in leading the music for worship.

Rehearsal can be a time of both preparation for worship and mentoring between generations. A church near our home uses contemporary music led by a praise band made up primarily of adults. For its Wednesday night service, however, middle-school and high-school students join the adults in leadership. These students have the opportunity to learn to lead worship, as well as to work with an adult mentor.

The use of technology for projecting words and music on screens can have benefits for congregational singing, but certain cautions are in order. It can be difficult for some to sing if only the words are projected. While some members learn music quickly by ear, others learn more easily if they have a printed musical staff in front of them. One solution is to supply printed copies of the music (in a songbook or hymnal, for example), as well as projecting the words (or perhaps both words and music) on a screen. This way we are being sensitive to those of all ages, as well as to those who have different learning styles. Many congregations, whether they use traditional or contemporary forms of worship, stand when they sing. Children and those who have difficulty standing may not be able to see the screen. In addition, long stretches of singing that involve standing can be difficult for some members; their needs should be considered in worship planning.

Litanies

Worship usually involves a lot of words—important words. They communicate specific messages about who God is, who we are, our relationship to God and to each other. Some of the words we use, though, can make it unnecessarily difficult for children to follow what we're doing. Craig Dykstra, vice president for religion at the Lilly Endowment, writes in *Growing in the Life of Faith* that finding the right words "involves the recovery of language that is clear enough to be comprehended by young people, rich enough to be meaningful, concrete enough to relate to the world as it is,

and critical enough to keep open the dynamics of inquiry and continuing conversation."[1] Karen Wilk, a youth advisor and now a
pastor of community life and discipleship in Edmonton, Alberta,
addresses this problem by suggesting that we should plan creative
calls to worship that "beckon not only adults but also children and
youth to come and meet with God, celebrate God's presence, and
respond to his love and Word with gratitude and action." She suggests that we use kid-friendly, attention-getting phrases like "God
calls all those with red hair and black . . ." or "the Lord calls all
who love playing basketball, swimming, and skiing to come and
worship Him . . ."[2]

Another way to make a liturgy more mindfully intergenerational is to employ childlike imagery. The following litany for
Christ the King Sunday, written by Carolyn Brown, a widely respected author and Presbyterian educator,[3] is childlike without being childish.

> Pastor: Like Jerusalem, O Christ, our sin must cause you to
> weep: For we confess, the things that make for peace are
> hidden from our eyes.
> Reader 1: God, sometimes I act like I am the king of the world. I
> try to make all the rules and break the ones I do not like, but
> People: *Yours is the kingdom, and the power, and the glory.*
> Reader 2: Lord, sometimes I act like I am the king of the world.
> I want to be the strongest so that I can get my way all the
> time, but
> People: *Yours is the kingdom, and the power, and the glory.*
> Reader 3: God, sometimes I act like I am the king of the world.
> I want everyone to listen to me, to watch me, to pay atten-
> tion to me and to tell me that I am wonderful, but
> People: *Yours is the kingdom, and the power, and the glory.*
> Reader 1: Forgive us, Lord. Help us to remember that you are
> the king, not us.
> Reader 2: Help us to serve you as our King.
> Reader 3: Help us to love one another, for
> People: *Yours is the kingdom, and the power, and the glory.*
> Pastor: For ever and ever. Amen.
> People: *For ever and ever. Amen.*

Trumpet Partners

Norma deWaal Malefyt

My father loved his trumpet. He played it well. But during the years of my growing up he rarely had time to play. I remember the Sunday-evening family hymn-sings in which we would encourage him to play with us for the "holy fun" of it.

When he retired, he made practice time a priority again—and then he regained his love to play in church, a desire that had lain dormant for many years. Until a few days before his sudden death at age 82, he would often be found as part of a musical ensemble playing in worship. Even the years couldn't mute his ability to play.

But he also loved to encourage others to play, especially youth, and he was eager to give them help and training.

On the last Sunday of his earthly life, the church's instrumental group was preparing to play for Easter Sunday—a few weeks away. His partner in the ensemble was a 12-year-old boy. My father encouraged him and wrote the transpositions that would enable an inexperienced musician to participate in worship leadership. It was special to see them sitting next to each other—trumpet partners—playing together in a way that said age doesn't matter. Eighty-two and twelve!

It's now eight years later, and I still receive comments about the unique and timeless partnership these two had.

The repetition of a line in a liturgy encourages younger children to learn the language of worship and to become involved in the service. Repetition and ritual are child-friendly. A liturgy repeated every Sunday can more easily include all participants than one that changes. If the pastor greets the congregation with "The Lord be with you" and the people answer "And also with you" every week, everyone knows when to participate and what to say.

Of course, many options are possible for incorporating repetition and ritual, even for churches that are not highly liturgical. For example, if your church has special worship times in the children's ministry, you can include some elements from the children's worship in congregational worship. Many of those worship centers greet the children with "The Lord be with you," but they also used the words of the *Shema:* "Hear, O Israel, the Lord our God is One." Incorporating these words into congregational worship helps children feel that their parents and other adult church friends worship the same way they do.

Liturgies can be simplified for children without losing their beauty. Here is a prayer of confession taken from the *Worship Sourcebook:*[4]

> God of Love, in the wrong we have done
> And in the good we have not done
> We have sinned in ignorance;
> We have sinned in weakness;
> We have sinned through our own deliberate fault.
> We are truly sorry. We repent and turn to you.
> Forgive us
> And renew our lives
> Through Jesus Christ, our Lord. Amen.

This prayer can be turned into a responsive reading and simplified like this:

> Leader: God of Love,
> *People: We have sinned.*
> Leader: In the wrong we have done,
> *People: We have sinned.*
> Leader: In the good we have not done,
> *People: We have sinned.*
> Leader: We are truly sorry.
> *People: Forgive us.*
> Leader: Make us new again.
> *People: Forgive us.*
> Leader: Through Jesus Christ, our Lord,
> *People: Amen.*

You could also ask children, teens, or adults to think about the sorts of sins they have committed. Make a list and insert that list of sins in the litany like this:

> Leader: For hitting our brother, for lying to our mother,
> People: Forgive us.
> Leader: For jumping on the bed, for not spending our money
>   the right way,
> People: Forgive us.
> Leader: For not praying, for treating our friends badly,
> People: Forgive us.

Congregations can also help many of us, not just children, understand the parts of worship by considering John Witvliet's concept of "vertical habits."[5] He points out that each of the parts of worship can be expressed in simple words, words that a toddler might use, words that are essentially *vertical* because they express our conversation with God. For example, one of the elements of worship is confessing our brokenness. That can be simply expressed as "I'm sorry." Witvliet's list of such phrases is short—only eight items: "I love you," "I'm sorry," "Why?," "I'm listening," "Help," "Thank you," "What can I do?," and "Bless you." These items convey all the parts of worship. What we do in worship can be expressed simply, so we should do our best to make our worship accessible to all church members. We're not suggesting that all of the rich language of worship should be eliminated, but we need to make sure, when we use words that will be unfamiliar to children and teens or to adults who are new Christians, that we unpack those words for them. This list of vertical habits is one place to start.

Simplifying the language can also give parts of our worship new meaning for all worshipers. Debbie Hough and Mary Speedy, two Presbyterian directors of education, suggest that an interesting exercise is to "rewrite the liturgy using action words (verbs) that clearly state what is to happen." So "hymns of praise" becomes "We sing praises to God" and "Prayer of Confession" becomes "We tell God what we have done wrong."[6]

Having lay members of the congregation read parts of a litany both expands the number of people who lead worship and brings new insights. On a recent Sunday our pastor asked us to find two teens to help read one of the litanies. We found Andrew and Nicole and sent them to the pastor as ready volunteers. Nicole's brother had just joined the Marines a few months earlier. Her family and our congregation are filled with joy at his achievements but also fearful that he may soon find himself in a danger. One of the lines that Nicole was selected to read was "May your kingdom come to those who suffer from wars." When Nicole read these lines, it brought an intensity to the lines that they would not have had if the pastor had read them. It changed this reading from something abstract to something very realistic, even jarring.

Another way to make litanies more engaging is to connect them to other church programs. When we noticed that a number of church-school classes were studying the Lord's Prayer, we asked the pastor to try to incorporate the Lord's Prayer into each service over the next few weeks. We created child-friendly litanies that used lines from the Lord's Prayer for various parts of the worship service. We also encouraged church-school teachers (for both children and adults) to pray the prayer in their classes and asked parents to teach it and to pray it together as a family. Saying the Lord's Prayer weekly in worship offers an ideal entry point for children's practices.

Scripture Readings

The reading of Scripture can be brought to life in worship, helping your congregation hear familiar passages in a new way. Dramatic readings of Scripture can, if done with care, be especially helpful and can offer an opportunity for intergenerational ministry. You can provide dramatic readings simply by matching the reader to the text—for example, a teenage girl and an older man can read the songs of Mary and Zechariah, or an older couple can read the story of Abraham and Sarah.[7] This idea can be taken a step further by presenting Scripture as drama. During Lent a group of men from one local church presented the trial of Jesus before the Sanhedrin dramatically to their congregation. The men who played the members of the Sanhedrin wore black robes, and the chief priest was in a decorated academic robe. While they didn't look like authentic first-century Jews, the simple costumes helped place them in the scene. The play used 14 men from the congregation. The children (and the adults too, for that matter) especially enjoyed seeing fathers and friends up-front acting out this story.

The Scripture lesson for the day can, of course, be read by a different member of the congregation each Sunday, including senior members, teens, and children. Remember, though, with all lay readers, to help them succeed. Go over the passage with the reader. Print the reading in a large font. Review any words he or she might stumble on or find difficult to pronounce. When we are working with young people, we emphasize that they have to think about the reading so that people will hear and understand. That means using pauses, and varying tone of voice to communicate nuances of meaning. Many readers need help in understanding how to speak through a microphone effectively. Sometimes just articulating some of the things that good oral readers do can make a huge difference for those who read aloud.

Other ideas for reading Scripture include responsive readings or choral readings. Even some parts of Scripture that don't easily lend themselves to dramatization, such as the Psalms or the Epistles, could be read responsively to enhance the impact. Michael Perry, an editor, did a fine job of dramatizing much of Scripture in his three-volume *Dramatized Bible*.[8] For narrative portions Perry merely used the words of Scripture with the "he said" or "she said" taken out, and assigned the parts to the characters. For the non-narrative sections he creatively split up the passages to allow for multiple readers. People in your congregation, perhaps an intergenerational team, could write this sort of dramatization, and then read it on Sunday. Here is a short example using Psalm 133:

> All: How very good and pleasant it is when kindred live to-
>   gether in unity!
> Reader 1: It is like the precious oil on the head,
> Reader 2: running down upon the beard, on the beard of Aaron,
> Reader 1: running down over the collar of his robes!

Reader 2: It is like the dew of Hermon, which falls on the
mountains of Zion!

All: For there the Lord has ordained the blessing, life for
evermore.

Advent Dance

AnnaMae Bush

One of the most cherished traditions at our church is recreated
each Advent. It began 20 years ago when a member choreo-
graphed two verses of "O Come, O Come, Emmanuel." This
processional dance portrays God's people burdened by captivity
and freed by Emmanuel.

Dressed in black and purple, male and female dancers from
age 5 to age 50 form a single lineup from 10 to 15 members long.
In order by height and with heads bowed, the dancers link hands
with those in front of and behind them at the back of the neck,
conveying the appearance of a chain gang.

While the congregation sings, they move ahead slowly in
rhythm with the music—three steps forward and one back, three
steps forward and one back . . . until the refrain. At "Rejoice,"
they lift their heads and raise their hands high in the air.

On verse 2 the motions of the dancers, from youngest to
oldest, are designed to portray the morning star dispelling the
shadows of the night and turning darkness into light. Once again
at the refrain, they raise their heads and hands and continue their
forward movement. After the singing ends, the piano continues
while the dancers link hands and move toward the back of the
sanctuary.

With movements so closely wedded to the text, the dance is
a poignant expression of Israel's grief and yearning that speaks
to the same emotions in our hearts today. And when both children and adults are included, this dance visually reminds us that
both are part of God's people and are affected by what happens
to one another.

Prayer

Praying together in worship is important in the life of the congregation, but in many churches the only voice heard during prayers is that of the pastor. That in itself is not a bad thing. Congregational prayer is that of the gathered people of God, and the person uttering the words does so on behalf of all present.

Nonetheless, it is good to have a variety of voices heard so that the people of God are reminded that these are the *prayers of the people* and not just of the pastor. Indeed, having elders lead in the congregational prayer not only adds other voices but also models shared leadership. Many prayers in worship are written and read. These written prayers could easily be read or written by other members of the congregation representing a wide range of ages.

At a worship conference Lynnae, a sixth-grader, was asked to write and read the prayer of confession for one worship services. Here is what she wrote:

Dear God,
You are a great and awesome God.
Today we come to you in a prayer of confession.
We are sorry for the many things that we have done that are
     wrong in your eyes.
We are also sorry for all the things we should have done but we
     didn't do.
We are asking now for forgiveness for these things,
And for other things that we have done wrong and don't even
     know about.
Please forgive us.
In your name alone we pray, Amen.[9]

This prayer was not part of a special children's worship service; it was used in a regular worship service for this conference, in which many generations were deliberately included as worship leaders. Lynnae's prayer showed that a child's voice could express the heart of an entire congregation. Lynnae was not asked to make up a prayer on the spot. She was asked ahead of time to think about what she wanted to say and to write it out. The worship leader went over it with her, and together they discussed how the service would go, and she practiced reading her prayer in the sanctuary. By the time of the service, Lynnae was ready to go, and while she may have been a little nervous, she knew what to do and did an excellent job.

You don't have to have a child pray, though, to make prayers child-friendly. Children's concerns should be expressed in prayer, no matter who leads. Remember special events in the lives of children in the congregation, such as the beginning or ending of the school year. Pray for safety on the playground, for sports teams, or for children's friendships. You can also help children understand the needs of people for whom the congregation prays. Brian, a friend of ours who was diagnosed with cancer, visited a children's worship class and talked with the children about his illness. When his name was mentioned in prayer during worship services, the children could more fully engage with the prayer because they knew Brian and his situation.

In *A Child Shall Lead* John Witvliet suggests that story prayers can help children connect the Bible stories that they hear at home and in church to their prayer life. Here is a prayer of praise that connects to familiar stories:

> We praise you, God,
> because you created the world, you saved your people Israel,
> you helped David when he was fleeing from Saul,
> you sent Jesus as a sign of your love.
> We praise you as the great God who did all these things.
> Amen.[10]

Prayers like this speak the praises of the entire congregation and yet help children hear the prayer in a way that engages them and invites them into worship. In his essay in the same book,[11] David Vroege, a pastor in Nova Scotia, has included a number of prayers that can be spoken by either adults or children. These simple but beautiful prayers can both enhance your worship and include people of all ages in leadership.

The Arts

Using the arts in worship can also enhance the experience for everyone while allowing people of various ages to work together. Music, of course, is the art form most commonly used in worship, but many others can also be drawn in. The visual arts have been used effectively for centuries, but many churches don't often invite congregation members to use their gifts in the visual arts to enhance worship. Bulletin covers can regularly feature the art or design work of church members. We often invite children to draw Nativity pictures for use in our Advent publications. If your church uses a projector in the sanctuary, art from the children or from any member of the congregation that reflects the Bible passage for the week can be projected before worship begins. Photos taken by children, teens, and adults can also be used.

Jack's Place at Faith Church

Mark Stephenson

"Pastor Herb" was getting burned out. He had served Faith Church well, but he needed some time away. So the council granted him a much-needed sabbatical rest. In his absence the members of the congregation recognized how much they appreciated his ministry. He was missed by the members of his congregation—including a special man named Jack.

Jack's first contact with Faith Church came through involvement in the Friendship group that met there. ("Friendship" helps churches share God's love with people who have cognitive impairments.) Jack couldn't drive, so he walked to church. At Friendship group, Jack learned about the love and fellowship and worship of church life. He wanted to become part of Faith Church too and was thrilled when he publicly professed his faith.

Jack attended worship nearly every Sunday. He made many friends at Faith Church, including Pastor Herb. He asked about Pastor Herb's absence every week at the Friendship group.

The church that our friend Amy attends has a series of windows that separate the worship space from the gathering space. Amy realized that those windows could well be used to represent the church seasons artistically, so she and another artist in the congregation enlisted elementary-school children to help them create the art for the windows. Under the helpful guidance of these artistically gifted adults, the children created beautiful but childlike pieces of art to help the congregation remember the changing of the church seasons. An artist in another church made markers and crayons available to all children during the church service and encouraged them to create something that reflected what the pastor said during the sermon. He also drew what he heard in the service; after church they all met with the pastor (and other interested people) to share what they had created and to reflect on what they had heard. Other art forms such as dance and theater can also be used in worship to give additional opportunities for younger people to connect with older members (see chapter 6).

The principle in all of these opportunities for connecting remains the same: to encourage people of all ages to be involved in preparation for worship or in leadership during the worship service. It is important that all people who do this, young or old, be helped to succeed. By partnering experienced people with novices, we are not only involving more people but also building a community and training a new generation of worship leaders. The ideas and examples presented here suggest steps on a journey to help your congregation develop a culture of being intergenerational, so that it can become a community in which children, teens, and adults work and worship together.

Discussion Questions

1. List ways that your church already connects generations in worship.

2. What are some areas of worship in which your church is not making connections?

3. Does music serve as a connector or a divider in your congregation? What could you do to begin to make it more of a connector?

4. Find a recent order of worship for your congregation. Is it accessible to children and teens? How could it be rewritten so that it would be more child-friendly?

5. How could your congregation set up mentoring relationships so that young people can learn to lead worship effectively?

Laura L. Keeley has more than 20 years of experience as a school and church educator and currently serves as director of children's ministries at a church in Holland, Michigan. Robert J. Keeley is an educator, professor of education at Calvin College, and chair of the Education Department. His most recent publication is Helping Our Children Grow in Faith: Nurturing the Spiritual Development of Kids. *The Keeleys have four children.*

CHAPTER 10

Worship Planning in a Church of All Ages

Norma deWaal Malefyt and Howard Vanderwell

After all has been written and discussed, the spotlight turns to those who are responsible for planning worship. Their task is considerably more complex if worship is to be accessible to all ages. This chapter addresses the task of worship planners. It's written by two people who have collaborated together in intergenerational worship planning for nearly 30 years. In this chapter you'll find them setting the stage by pointing to the planning structures and processes that need to be in place, and then zeroing in on the most specific intergenerational concerns for planning.

If you are a worship planner, pastor, or musician, you might be feeling somewhat anxious by what you have read and heard so far. You've heard authors say we face new and complex issues in the church today. You've heard them say there are good biblical reasons for wanting to hold the generations together as they worship. You've been able to take an inside look at the delicate process of faith development in children and youth. You've heard that a ministry of developing faith takes a whole new way of thinking and seeing, a new culture. You've observed from a large congregation that simply changing the worship style won't quickly make it intergenerational. You've been pointed to many places in worship and the life of the congregation where old and young can remain connected. You've heard that we should resurrect the lost art of storytelling, and that the sermon should be marked by "chatting," "gossiping," and "daydreaming."

Perhaps you want to nod your head in assent, and then your heart wants to run away from a task so complex.

But we suggest that there is another way to respond, a more healthy and positive way. We see a fascinating challenge to draw out your best, a plowing-new-ground adventure that requires healthy group efforts, and an outstanding opportunity to effect worship renewal in congregations around the world.

Fix this picture in your mind—congregations of old and young reaching across their age differences as they meet together with God. Visualize worship services of praise and prayer, song and sacrament, sermon and service, that are accessible to all ages. See a teenager singing heartily with her grandfather, both carefully learning the other's songs. Imagine a parent and child thrilled to come to the Lord's Table together. See and hear a young boy and his middle-aged aunt standing in front, jointly leading in prayer. It's the biblical "daydream" of "young men and women alike, old and young together!" (Ps. 148:12) being lived out before your very eyes.

With that vision and sense of adventure firmly fixed in your mind and heart, thank God that you have the privilege of applying your gifts to the significant task of shaping worship for your congregation. You are participating with Christ in his work of bringing the new creation.

So what will it take? And how should you proceed? Before we can talk about the specifics of how to be intergenerational, we'll have to get the basic structure in place.

Team Organization

Usually weekly worship services are planned by teams of people who have a variety of gifts and insights, except in smaller congregation where the task may have to be done by one. For this task to remain in the hands of only one person, however, for any period of time will easily produce staleness, burnout, and, likely, worship services that are marked by sameness.

Congregations employ several models to create teams of worship planners. Your team may be made up of staff members, or the pastor and a key musician, either paid or volunteer. If you are a pastor, we encourage you to seek out the main musicians in your congregation and perhaps mentor them in the art of planning. Some churches use a planning team of volunteers who meet weekly. Some modify this arrangement by having multiple planning teams that rotate weekly, monthly, or seasonally. In other congregations the team is marked by a partnership between staff members and a committee of volunteers who meet less often than weekly. In any case, in addition to a core planning team, you'll need supplementary people who will serve as liaisons with music groups and various age groups.[1] Bear in mind that your church may be at a different stage from others in the process of putting a structure in place. If you are just beginning, you'll have to start by organizing your efforts, writing some guidelines, and looking for appointees or volunteers. If you have more experience, you may want to move to a new phase in your planning and give specific attention to intergenerational sensitivities.

The selection of your team should be given careful thought. Often a planning team is made up of about a half-dozen members—according to group dynamics, about the right size. Our conversations with churches verify this number. All members of the planning team should be in agreement on the basic understanding of worship. A common commitment to the biblical teachings about worship will provide a forum in which efforts can be focused on planning and not on debates about the fundamentals. A planning team should not spend its time engaged in weekly debates about divergent understandings of worship.

The members of this planning team should generally be representative of the various generations in the congregation. Although you need not rigidly require a member from each decade of life, planning worship services that will be accessible to all generations will go better when the planners generally represent a variety of ages. It may be good to include high-school youth and those who are sensitive to the experiences of high-school youth, but for younger children it is better to include mentoring efforts with younger children, including them in preparation for worship rather, and worship leadership.

Each member of the planning team should be marked by sensitivity to the needs of the various generations. All must be willing to step outside their own generational experiences, and to recognize and live into the needs and experiences of other generations. They must be people who listen to others, empathize with others' experiences, and reflect together on the experiences of all. Regular safeguards, such as a rotation of membership, are needed to retain good sensitivity. All of us can become stagnant after a while. While some members, such as staff, should remain as standing members of the team, others will likely be rotated in two- or three-year terms.

Team Activities

Once your team is in place and ready to work, team members will find that they have plenty to do. Worship services come rapidly, week after week. Most of those who participate will be laypeople with many other responsibilities, so efficiency and a good use of time are important. A group that understands its tasks clearly will enjoy its work and do it better.

Administration

A worship team has several primary tasks. The annual worship schedule will need to be established at the beginning of a worship season. A master worship calendar can be produced, and each member should have a copy. This annual worship calendar will note not only all Sundays, but also the seasons of the Christian Year and other special worship observances during the year. This is the time to watch for events that will provide opportunities to be intergenerational. The pastor will "plan in" series of sermons and the passages from the lectionary.

A wise planning team will also regularly evaluate worship services, with a particular eye to intergenerational concerns. Each congregation should identify a helpful set of criteria to use as evaluative tools to test whether its worship life is remaining accessible to all generations. All of us find it easy to slip into a comfortable pattern and to lose our willingness or objectivity to ask the hard questions about whether we are achieving the goal we set. If your group periodically spends some time trying to describe a genuinely intergenerational worship service, you'll be a long way toward evaluating your own.

Relationships

Worship planners cannot afford to be isolated from people. Indeed, success will often be shaped by communication and collaboration.

Do planners speak regularly with the pastor about his or her preaching and preaching plans? These conversations should take place in a trusting environment where all can be candid and comfortable together. The discussions should focus not only on the subjects being planned, but also on the accessibility of preaching for all ages (see chapter 7).

Others in the congregation also need to be part of the picture. Directors and leaders of children's and youth ministries will need to be consulted, both for their suggestions and for the sake of involving the youth in leadership roles. Directors of choral groups or ensembles should be involved early in the planning process. And don't forget about those who coach others in preparing readings, dramas, stories, dance, and other activities. To be sure, not everything has to be included in every service; balance and variety are important. Planners who fail to cultivate all these relationships well will lose the great benefits collaboration can provide; those who use them will be enriched.

Good planners need to gather the gifted and willing volunteers who can serve as worship leaders, though some may need help in developing those gifts. A volunteer resource bank becomes a goldmine for those who plan (See appendix A for a sample). Some congregations have a sign-up of such volunteers at the beginning of each season.[2] As you develop a resource list of ready volunteers, determine where coaching and rehearsing are necessary. Some are ready to serve in worship leadership; others will need help. In dance, drama, storytelling, and music, rehearsals are not only necessary but expected. However, for parts such as prayers and readings, rehearsals need to be encouraged. It is often helpful to practice reading, making sure all can hear clearly, that the microphone is used properly, and that the reading interprets the nuances of the passage. In addition, we suggest developing mentoring and apprenticeships for children and youth. In each congregation most children and youth would welcome help in discovering their gifts and entering leadership roles.

The ethos of intergenerational worship will be encouraged by conversations that serve as bridges to connect the generations. Perhaps a sermon discussion group after the service on Sunday morning can be planned so that youth and adults can talk together about the sermon and the liturgy over "Dew," coffee, and cookies. Or perhaps small groups of adults and young people can meet informally to share their experiences and insights about living the Christian life. Anything that promotes relationships across age barriers will aid worship that aims to do the same.

Creative Planning

Now you are ready to plan. Your structure is in place. Your committee is organized. You have the worship schedule in everyone's hands. You have good communication with others who are involved. You have a good idea of whom you can count on as lay leaders. And you have all ages in view. Now it's on to the liturgy that must be designed—an intergenerational liturgy. The degree of designing that you do will depend on whether you use the lectionary, have a more-or-less set liturgy, or have greater openness to a somewhat different liturgy each week.

You have the Scripture and the title of the pastor's sermon, so your first steps are taken toward formulating the theme for the service. It will help your planning to express the theme of the service in a crisp, brief statement. Be thinking already at this point of how different age groups will relate to this theme. Make it accessible to all, or at the very least be thinking now about how the parts of the service could draw each age in. For instance, if your theme is "We are secure in God's love," you may begin to plan the liturgy thinking about how children and adolescents, parents and empty nesters and seniors all need security in different ways. You may think how the concept of "security" will mean different things to each age level. And then you may start to think how readings, songs, prayers, and other art can express the theme in a way that relates to each generation represented.

Then it's time to identify the elements of the liturgy and how they can be designed to fit your theme. Write (and at times, re-write) prayers of confession that are age-inclusive. Then select some supplementary Scripture readings that will reinforce the

Family Sign-ups

Mary Elder

In our church the word "intentional" is key. The leadership team is always looking for ways to integrate worship into all of life. Our mission statement says, "As a body of believers, we will glorify God by calling others to Christ, nurturing all persons, growing in faith and serving in love."

Our leadership team distributes a form on which members (children, teens, and adults) indicate which ministries they want to serve in for the following year. Last year each form had two options for each ministry: male or female. It provided opportunity for a husband and wife to fill out the same form and serve together.

However, this year, to deliberately encourage family worship, the leadership team modified the form. The new form has three options: male, female, or family. *Families* (sometimes three generations) signed up to bring music into worship, perform in worship skits, read Scripture, greet members before worship, carry in banners or light candles, usher, and pray with the pastor before the service starts.

By simply changing one part of the sign-up form, the leadership team made it easier for families to think about ways they could love and honor God together. We find that we have promoted family discussion about worship and have fostered the worship leadership of multiple generations.

theme. Outline the intercessory prayer with an ear and eye for the struggles and concerns of the old and the young. Select songs that can engage all. At times the young will stretch to learn the favorites of the seniors; at other times the seniors may work to learn some of the songs of the young. One will hope that all are learning to be open and willing to learn new hymns and songs, because you have stressed the importance of sharing things in common. The anthems and ensembles can be located in the liturgy where they best serve the flow of the service, depending on their content and the progress of thought in the service. Be thinking about the transitions that are needed and, if others besides the pastor are leading, who will make them within the service so that all elements are held together.

If your congregation celebrates the Lord's Supper every week, then you are accustomed to including the sacrament in all your worship planning. However, if your congregation schedules the sacrament less often, you will want to give extra effort to integrating it carefully into the flow of the service. As you plan, ask questions about how each age will be included. How can the welcome to the table be given so that it speaks equally to all ages? If children are welcomed at the table, will they experience hospitality in the same manner as adults? If children are not welcomed to full participation at the table, how can they receive a blessing so that they will not feel that they are only spectators? And will the congregation be reminded that the picture of all ages coming to the table is a biblical expression of the body of Christ? If communicants come forward to be served, how can you accommodate those who are less mobile and less steady? Will there be music while worshipers are receiving the sacrament? How could the music reflect the faith-journey of each age? Knowing there are different stages of faith development (chapter 3), how does one balance what is a necessary expression for one generation with what is a "growing into" for another?

Similarly, how will your planning team design baptismal services? When you plan a service for the baptism of an infant, will you be able to integrate it meaningfully into the entire liturgy so that the welcome of Christ speaks to all ages present? And when an adult is baptized, will this be a community event in which all ages welcome this new Christian? Will it be a time for some to anticipate their own baptism? Will the welcome speak the language of all ages? Will children be encouraged to think about their baptism? Will adults be encouraged to remember theirs? Let your planning team spend some time thinking of how a worship service in an intergenerational setting can be the ideal time and location for all the members of the body of Christ to remember their own baptisms and to reaffirm their baptismal vows—which may have been 10 years ago or 50. Ask how we can be made more aware of the agelessness of our baptism and our baptismal vows.

In all your planning keep these questions on your "front burner": How will all ages be able to relate to this? How will this speak to all groups within the congregation? Ask these questions frequently in your planning sessions so that an intergenerational concern is integrated into all your planning.

A Tool Kit for Planners

Imagine that your planning now is well underway. The liturgy is taking shape, and you are hopeful that it will be accessible to all. Your planning team is buoyed up by the group energy that is generated by the richness of your collaborative efforts. And yet, you sense that other areas beyond the liturgy need attention. So you all push your chairs back a little and begin to brainstorm about everything that Sunday will involve. After a somewhat slow start (as brainstorming often goes), your thoughts pick up speed, and the ideas flow faster. Your chairperson is writing them on the board as fast as you can mention them all. And the secretary is generating a computer file at the same time (You don't want to lose valuable ideas.) Every member is soon saying, "What about . . . ?" "Should we consider . . . ?" and "I wonder if . . . ?" When all is said and done, here's your list:

- An order of worship that children can follow and understand.
- A sermon outline with easy words on it.
- Another sermon outline for middle-school children.

- A bulletin for children with fill-in-the-blanks ideas about the service.
- Posters in the narthex that have been designed by children.
- Banners in the sanctuary designed by artists of the congregation.
- Children's classes that use motions with the Creed and the Lord's Prayer.
- Youth (and adults) who will dance while the congregation sings.
- A reader's group to read the Scripture passage.
- A choir of adults and children, or a male chorus, or a female chorus, or a mixed group.
- An intercessory prayer led by a grandparent and grandchild side by side.
- A wide age range among the lay leaders at any service.
- A family choir including parents, children, youth, and grandparents (and singles who are part of the church family).
- A soundproof "cry room" attached to the sanctuary for parents with fussy children.
- Rocking chairs with quilts in the back row for parents and infants.
- A Hearing LOOP system for the benefit of those whose hearing is limited.
- Large-print editions of all worship sheets, songs, and sermon outlines.
- Several pews cut short to accommodate wheelchairs in the middle of the sanctuary.

Wow, that had to be about the most stimulating 20 minutes ever spent in your meeting. We're sure other groups could continue to add more to the list. When you turn to your own situation, you'll want to be selective about these, because not all will fit each congregation, and surely you will want to add some of your own.

So the next week, you do it again, except that this time you focus on special events in your worship life that would engage all generations. Again, after a somewhat slow start, your ideas began rolling. "Maybe we should have . . ."

- A youth service where our youth draw us into praying for their needs . . .
- A seniors' service where youth are asked to pray with and for them . . .
- A service about the demands of parenting so that others will understand . . .
- A service about singles that enables others to recognize their needs . . .
- A Children's Ministry Sunday to celebrate all the growth of faith . . .
- A series of services on the "chapters of life" (see appendix B) . . .
- A service to remember our baptisms, whether we are old or young . . .
- A service to give thanks for the lives of those who have died this year . . .
- A service of prayers for healing . . .
- A mission emphasis to celebrate intergenerational service projects . . .

So you all went home from your meeting that evening with the fascinating awareness that the worship life of your congregation could become more exciting and relevant than you ever dreamt before.

Partnering with Parents

You are right on target if you are realizing that to succeed in planning worship that is genuinely intergenerational, the parents in the congregation are key people. God has intended them to be the primary shapers of their children's lives—from birth. So although you are concerned about all ages, you realize that it is necessary to give special attention to formative worship in the lives of children and youth. As you think about that, you begin to realize more and more that you and the parents are partners. You need them; they need you.

Debra Rienstra, a professor of English at Calvin College, tells the story of a woman who described her childhood in her Roman Catholic congregation, going to Latin mass weekly with her father and her sister. None of the adults had ill intentions, but neither her father, nor the priests, nor the lay leaders in the parish ever did much to explain to her what the mass could mean and why it was important. "As a result, the whole operation was an exercise in missed opportunities."[3] Here was a failure of partnership. Such a story can probably be repeated by many. In comparing and evaluating our own experiences, both of us realized we had experienced some of the same. Our parents meant well and were careful to stress the value of faithful church attendance, and they combined it with faithful Bible reading at mealtimes. We were taught by example that obedience in such matters was important. But neither of us was given any instruction, either about why we were reading the Bible, or about why and how we should worship. We were expected to be obedient and faithful; understanding it all was quite another thing. Much of our learning was accomplished through "spiritual osmosis" and seemingly unintentional mentoring.

Today, if worship is going to be genuinely intergenerational, we'll have to put extra efforts into making our worship conversations at home helpful. Parents will need to take a more intentional leading role. Yet many parents are unprepared for this task; they feel unskilled at explaining worship and find themselves unsure of how to approach the matter. So partnership with worship leaders will be necessary.

Parents should be given encouragement and aid so that they can teach the fundamentals about worship at home. Rich is the home where parents are able to explain to their children that worshiping is much like having a conversation with someone, except that this time it's God. Help them imagine a conversation with God that goes something like this:

"*Welcome; it's good to see you.*"
"I love you."

"You are mine and I care for you."
"I'm sorry when I do wrong."
"I am always ready to forgive you."
"I need your help, and my friends do, too."
"Here is my word for you today."
"Thank you, what can I do?"
"I bless you."
"I will see you again."

Each part of worship should be explained in language that a child can understand, and the flow of worship presented as a conversation so that children and youth can grasp what is happening.[4] Perhaps some of these concepts could be introduced in children's moments within worship so that parents can reinforce them at home in conversation around the dinner table.

Another element of this task for parents involves teaching children the terms used in worship.

- What is *praise* and why do we do it?
- What does it mean to *confess*?
- What is a *litany*?
- What is a *sermon* and why is it always about the Bible?
- Why do we *pray*? And do we know that God hears us?
- Why do we *sing*?
- What is a *benediction* and why does the pastor give it?
- Why does *baptism* have water?
- Why do we have wafers (or bread) at the *Eucharist*? And why juice (or wine)?

A home where there are periodic conversations about these terms is a place where healthy worshipers and future leaders can be formed.

Parents will do well to help their children prepare for worship when Sunday morning or evening comes. Some of those efforts will be immediate—preparation for today's worship—and some will be more long-term. A home where the Bible is read regularly sets a good pattern for worshiping. A conversation about the fact that we can expect to celebrate Palm Sunday, or have the Lord's

Supper, or hear testimonies this morning will help all prepare well. A leisurely schedule makes it easier to do such teaching; a mad dash to church will not provide good teaching time.

There is a special joy in watching parents practice in-the-pew training during the worship service. A father running his finger along the lines of words in the hymnal, Bible, or printed litany is doing on-the-job training. Allowing children to turn to the Bible or hymnal page draws generations together in worship. Making sure children have clear sight lines to what is projected on a screen is vital. Seeing their parents writing sermon notes teaches young children something about worship. A parent's posture in prayer and in receiving a blessing also teaches them. If some element of the worship service seems different this week, a whispered conversation about what it means will bring great benefits.

Certainly what happens after the worship service will either positively reinforce good worship or seriously undermine it. We all know that children and youth pick up attitudes from their parents. The habit of making critical comments in the car on the way home will clearly play a part in forming the attitudes of others in the

Every Member Is a Minister

Anne Zaki

I think back to my home congregation often, and I see it as a model of what the church ought to be. It is located in an extremely poor neighborhood at the heart of downtown Cairo, Egypt. Though the congregation numbers 25 families, it serves 200 children and 150 adults through education and outreach ministries. It is a transient congregation because people move out as soon as they have done better for themselves. Therefore the congregation needs constantly to be training ministry leaders.

The congregation's motto is "Every Member Is a Minister." Every person, including all ages and gifts, becomes involved in and committed to a specific area of ministry. Often one started bearing responsibilities in the church at the age of 8 or 10, and those responsibilities grew with age. The training was like that family. A negative attitude in one generation will almost always be reproduced in the next. However, affirming conversations about what was special and thrilling this morning will reinforce attitudes that provide fertile soil for good worship habits. A parent's explanation of what helped him or her to pray particularly well today will go far in forming a child's attitude.

The partnership between parents and leaders is seldom recognized for as powerful as it is, or could be. Leaders should work to reinforce this partnership.

Educational Efforts

Most worship planners focus exclusively on their weekly work of planning and leading worship. Important as that is, we must understand that we also have an educational task. In all likelihood we have thought through worship and its issues more than most worshipers. We, however, want them to walk with us in growing into vital and enriching worship. For this to happen, we

of an apprentice with hands-on supervised ministry. By the time a person was in high school, ready to commit to full membership in the church, serving in various ministry capacities was like second nature.

I remember my first ministry of setting up snacks for Sunday school classes when I was 8, then helping the 5-years-olds with crafts when I was 10. At age 12, I was among a group of three girls receiving training to lead worship and public prayers during our weekly youth-group meetings, and at age 14, the church organist groomed me to play the piano at worship services by insisting that I sit next to him on the bench and watch what he did and listen to the cues from the pastor and the congregation. Every effort, whether excellent or lacking, was always received with encouragement and appreciation by the whole congregation. This experience provided me with an early affirmation that I've carried with me for many years as I found my way into full-time ministry.

must recognize the interconnectedness between our leadership, our planning, and the learning process on the part of the congregation. On Sunday we lead worship; during the week we plan worship; but for our work to be received well by the congregation, we must be educating the congregation about worship. Today, as new issues are raised in congregations about worship, the educational task in the congregation is a large one. To neglect or ignore it will undermine our efforts.

Many of our previous comments have focused on the training of children and youth for worship. We must not leave the impression that we believe that's the whole picture. Look more broadly at your congregation, and start with your leaders. How well do your congregational leaders understand what worship is? How many of your board of elders or deacons could define what worship is? How many of them understand the issues of worship renewal that are under discussion in the church around the world today? How about the leaders of your children's and youth ministries? How well do they understand worship? Are there any efforts to teach worship in their curricula? Perhaps all congregational leaders could benefit from a regular study of worship. Look at how the church today is experiencing crosswinds of worship preferences and new fads, often producing intense debates. Excellent resources for learning are available, some new and some tried and true. Leaders in these times need to be well informed about such issues.

But adult members need training too. Because we all encounter numerous ideas, convictions, preferences, and opinions about worship today, letting a congregation continue its routines without a plan for education in worship is asking for trouble. So how can we learn about worship together? Let's talk together about it in Sunday school classes for both adults and children, in adult education forums, on retreats, and in youth group discussions. We have participated in the educational plan of a congregation that held a series of Sunday-morning classes for adults and youth, mingled together, so that they not only studied worship together but also had opportunity to discuss their questions together. We have also engaged congregations in intergenerational Saturday-morning worship workshops that were open to all.

So what should you study? So many topics could be explored! Let's go back into another brainstorming session. Where do we start?

- Study the worship in the Old Testament and the New Testament.
- Study how worship has developed historically.
- Examine the understanding and definition of worship that your denomination or family of churches has developed.
- Discuss a book on worship and share new insights together.
- Examine the pattern of worship services of your congregation, and ask why that pattern is usually followed.
- Examine the terms used in worship, and be sure that everyone understands them.
- Spend a session re-examining the rich practice of baptism.
- Spend another session on the Lord's Supper and all of its valuable symbolism.
- Study the Christian Year and see the valuable rhythm of worshiping through the entire cycle of Christ's ministry.
- Study the purpose of Advent, Epiphany, Lent, Easter, and Pentecost—maybe in preparation for celebrating these seasons.
- Ask why your worship space is designed the way it is.
- Reflect on the visual aspects of worship. What symbols are present in your worship space? Is there a baptismal font? A Lord's Table? What other architectural or decorative elements, or other visuals, are present to direct worshipers' thoughts? How could art and visuals aid our worship?
- Look at the songs of worship—why do you sing the songs you do? What are the songs that will last a lifetime and which songs speak only for the present time?
- Gather a group and study worship together at a worship conference or symposium.

While you are learning together as a congregation, include some face-to-face conversations with strategic worship leaders. How about a question-and-answer session with your pastor about

Merely Cute or Deeply Profound?

Jan Zuidema

For many the annual Christmas program brings back mental pictures of simple affairs with nervous kids, beaming parents, shepherds in Aunt Ruth's old turquoise bathrobe, and wise men fortunate enough to wear the fake velvet robes. Now many congregations mount pageants that could rival an evening at the Met with costumes, stage lighting, and perhaps even a descending angel.

No one would have thought of laughing, applauding, or taking our picture in our dragging bathrobes, because you didn't do that in church. Now applause and the "Kodak moment" happen often. I wonder if we could be missing how our children are trying to lead us by confusing performance and worship.

The children in our congregation participate in a youth chorale/liturgical dance group. They sing, sign, and dance, helping

his work in leading worship and preaching? And a panel discussion with your congregation's worship planners? And with the musicians in your congregation? It might be instructive for some to observe a sample worship planning session. For instance, give them Ephesians 2:8-10, and let them work together on finding songs, readings, an anthem, and prayers that would be fitting for such a worship service.

You may see planning and leading worship as your primary task, but whatever you do to raise the awareness and understanding of your congregation members about worship and the issues of worship will be a valuable investment in the worship life of your congregation.

Thoughtful Change

While we are thinking about teaching the congregation, let us admit what all of us are probably thinking right now. How can we to interpret and deepen our worship experience. At rehearsal one week, one of the children asked if they would be "good enough" on the following Sunday for the worshipers to applaud as they occasionally do for the adult choir.

When our children participate in worship, they usually do so with intensity and innocence—intensity because they are somewhat unskilled in liturgy and song, trying hard to get their part in worship "right," and innocence because they are still waiting to be trained in worship habits. However, when our responses signal to them that we expect them to be "cute" rather than an intrinsic part of the drama of worship, we may have missed their contribution to the dialogue between God and God's people. Our responses to what we perceive as "cuteness" may seem appropriate at the time but may cheapen their contributions and miss the point entirely. Our children are never "merely cute." They are taking their place in deeply and profoundly telling the glorious story of salvation.

avoid debate, argument, and conflict? Not all agree on everything. And change in worship is a reality today. How can we walk our way through that maze or minefield and still keep the generations intact? How can we have difficult conversations that are also healthy, both in the planning team and in the congregation?

It's not hard to see that change is difficult for a congregation under most circumstances, but changing worship in a congregation committed to keeping the generations together is even more complex. The educational task, therefore, will also encompass helping a congregation recognize and implement change that is, above all, thoughtful. Thoughtful change has several key ingredients:

1. The need for change is recognized.
2. The benefit of change is clearly set forth.
3. All options are carefully examined and explained.
4. Communication is open and thorough.
5. A high level of trust among the members of the group is constantly fostered.

It is also necessary to remember that the pace of change must be manageable and not rushed. The planners and leaders of the congregation carry a large responsibility to foster an environment where thoughtful change can occur.

To encourage such an environment three virtues must be cultivated—discernment, humility, and patience. Wise worship leaders value all three.

Discernment is a fruit of the Holy Spirit's work in one's life. The exercise of discernment requires that we be informed, observant, and able to distinguish between principles and personal preferences. Discerning people are aware of abiding truth and principles that must not be violated, and are able to rise above personal prejudices to make objective evaluations. They are able to distinguish between what is unchangeable and what is transient. Discernment also involves a sense of which changes will be acceptable to a congregation and which will be offensive. A discerning person is usually a steadying influence in a group discussion. Such a person will be able to draw the necessary lines between what is wise and unwise, what may be acceptable and what will be offensive. Not everyone is equally discerning; when your group recognizes someone who is, value his or her leadership.

The gift of humility is a virtue cultivated in the mature Christian heart so that "winning" a debate or argument is not necessary. The humble person is more interested in serving the welfare of the whole group than in his or her own agenda. When a humble person is part of a group discussion, you will find that she is able to set her own personal preferences aside for the sake of the welfare of the whole. She will not doggedly cling to her own favorite ideas, but will quietly listen to others, learn from all discussion, and support what will serve the welfare of the group even if it means giving up her own preference. This person will never sacrifice principle but will relinquish a favored choice. The center for such members is not themselves but the group. They are good people to have in any discussion.

Patience, in Scripture, can mean the ability either to remain faithful and persistent even when obstacles appear, or to allow enough time to pass for a process to take place without undue haste. Both dimensions are necessary and helpful if a worship leader is to be a blessing to the congregation. We must be faithful and persistent even when the task is more difficult than we expected. Leaders who quickly give up or quit do not serve the congregation well. But we must also be willing to allow time to pass. Some tasks take time, much more time than we would like. This is especially true of worship change. Forcing it can cause division and discord. Allowing it to occur at a healthy and patient pace will generally create better acceptance. Planners who model these virtues in their work together will likely find the same spirit permeating much of the congregation.

The worship life of our congregations will usually be marked by change, to one degree or another. Some changes will take place comfortably; some will likely be divisive. Those who plan and lead worship would be wise to care for the spirit of the congregation as it experiences change. Educational efforts to help the congregation grow in its understanding of worship are necessary. Managing change is also important in a congregation of all ages. Leaders are the key to how well congregations are able to manage change. Respect and value deeply those worship leaders who serve their congregations and enable them to change thoughtfully.

So where does all of this bring us? We have come face to face with the fact that the task of worship planners is broader than normally perceived. Yes, they plan weekly worship services. And they are often involved in leading worship. But their work is broader. They also spend time trying to be creative in planning. They partner with parents to prepare a new generation. They provide educational opportunities for both leaders and the whole congregation. And they model virtues of discernment, humility, and patience.

They are key people in the life of the congregation.

Discussion Questions

1. What model for planning does your congregation have? Is it clear to others? Does it serve your cause effectively? Is the membership representative of all age groups in the congregation?

2. Evaluate the relationships between your planning group and other leaders in the congregation. Is communication open? Trusting? Timely?

3. Do you have a template that you follow in your worship planning? Does it include each of the necessary elements of worship? Evaluate how well it aids your planning and how well it reflects your congregation's theology of worship.

4. Have you ever spent time brainstorming as described in this chapter? If so, discuss your reactions to the process. If you haven't done it, how could it be beneficial?

5. How much education in worship matters has been provided in your congregation during the past few years? Is that adequate? How should it be improved?

6. Discuss the three virtues presented at the close of this chapter. Identify where they have been helpful in your work. Which one needs to be cultivated more?

Norma deWaal Malefyt is a musician who has served as director of music and as a church organist in a number of congregations. She currently teaches organ and keyboard skills in the Music Department of Calvin College. Howard Vanderwell has been senior pastor of four congregations during the years of his ministry, and is currently adjunct professor of worship at Calvin Theological Seminary. Both were church staff members together and have been working collaboratively as worship planners for nearly 30 years. Currently both are staff members at the Calvin Institute of Christian Worship in Grand Rapids, Michigan. They are co-authors of Designing Worship Together: Models and Strategies for Worship Planning.

Epilogue

Howard Vanderwell

With the eye of my heart, I can see them now, congregations that are ageless. Oh, they have all ages in their pews, right next to each other. But they never consider one age or generation to be more important than another. They value old and young alike. They give nurture for the new in the faith as well as the seasoned. They know and understand that every chapter of life's journey has its own particular needs and struggles, and so they aim to provide help for all. They understand that God is equally interested in meeting a child or an adult.

And so these congregations design their worship with a steady eye on each generation, and in so doing they draw all the age groups together in worship and teach each to value and listen to the others.

And as I watch them I discover . . .

- A congregation where planning intergenerational worship is not a negotiated compromise to keep everybody happy, but an expression of the new world Christ came to bring.
- A family whose noontime conversation on Sunday involves a parent-child dialogue about where each heard God speaking most clearly this morning.
- A father whispering to his children in explanation of what the pastor will be doing at the Lord's Table this morning.
- An intercessory prayer that includes thoughts about the playground, the office, the hospital, and the senior center.
- A congregation where the birth of a baby and the death of a saint are treated as equally notable events.

- A sanctuary where the 11-year-old and the 64-year-old are able to participate together despite very different cognitive abilities.
- A place where old and young are telling their stories of God's acts to each other on a regular basis.
- A preacher who intentionally seeks to know the culture of those who are much older and younger than she is.
- A worship planning team of all ages, with no member interested in winning but all concerned about a vital and healthy congregation.
- A congregation in which the children sing two songs in Sunday school each week that will be sung in the worship service, and in which worship planners select music so that some songs are familiar to children.
- A rural congregation of 85 worshipers that no longer feels inferior because of its limited resources, but rejoices as the retirees and the schoolchildren sit next to each other in their pews.
- A litany read by a 19-year-old girl and her 71-year-old grandfather, side by side.
- A preacher who speaks relationally and conversationally to the entire church family seated before him.
- A mixed choir that includes middle-school youth, high-school youth, and older adults.
- A pew in which a grandmother sits with her children and grandchildren and holds the hymnal for her grandson.
- A worship planning team that takes time during its planning session to explain to the 12th-grader what the term "Eucharist" means.
- A planning team that is a safe forum where people can explore their differences and disagreements while loving their work of planning.
- A congregation where one will never hear someone talk about children as a distraction or a nuisance.
- A congregation whose preacher meets with the youth group regularly to discuss worship and to listen to their suggestions of subjects and passages to preach on.

- A church gathering space where adults, teens, and children regularly talk together comfortably.
- In short, a worshiping congregation whose members sense that their togetherness expresses the pattern of the church worshiping in heaven.

Is it just a dream? I think not. It's the body of Christ functioning as the Lord of the church has in mind. If the pages of this book have helped us move more closely to this, then they will have served Christ and the church well.

Sample Worship Resource Bank

The following survey is made available to you as a sample for use in your own setting. We distributed it to the congregation each September as a new season began. Worshipers completed this survey as part of the offertory, and they were encouraged to consider the offering of their gifts and abilities to God and his church. The results were carefully tabulated, and a careful effort was made to include everyone who indicated a willingness to serve. Where additional assistance was needed, coaching was provided.

Worship Resource Bank Survey

The Worship Planning Team of our congregation aims to include laypeople in worship leadership. We want to practice the biblical principle of the priesthood of all believers. God delights to engage his people in conversation with him in worship.

Worship is not done *for* the people as though they were spectators, but *by* the people of God as their corporate offering of adoration and praise to him.

We solicit volunteers, young and old, male and female, who are willing to see this role of leadership as part of their ministry to the body of Christ. A commitment should be made for one entire year, and all volunteers will serve under the supervision of the Worship Planning Team.

Since we begin with a new list each season, please note that those who signed up last year must sign up again. If more than one person is using this form, please write your names in to identify which person is volunteering for each task.

If you have questions, or if you desire a copy of our worship guidelines, please read the brochure "Worship Life" in our literature rack, or contact either the pastor or the director of music.

Your Name _____

Please check your area of interest; you may indicate multiple areas of involvement.

Liturgy

☐ I'd be willing to participate in litanies and Scripture readings.
☐ I'd be willing to lead in readings and prayers with the Advent candles this season.
☐ I'd be willing to participate in a drama Scripture reading for worship.
☐ I'd be willing to coach an occasional Scripture drama group.
☐ I'd be willing to lead in prayer.
☐ I'd be willing to provide a children's message.

Vocal Music

☐ I'd be willing to participate as a soloist (circle the appropriate vocal range).

soprano   alto   tenor   bass

☐ I'd be willing to participate as part of a theme choir, such as a family choir, women's group, men's group, couples ensemble, etc.

Instrumental Music

☐ I'd be interested in serving as an accompanist or providing an offertory.
☐ I'd like to be considered for the bell choir as openings become available.
☐ I'm willing to participate in a small instrumental ensemble: Instrument played _____
☐ I'm willing to serve as an instrumental soloist.

Occasional Ensembles

☐ I'd be willing to participate in an ensemble:
  ☐ middle-school vocal
  ☐ high-school vocal
  ☐ trumpet
  ☐ flute
  ☐ string

Music Administration

☐ I'd be willing to serve as a music librarian.
☐ I'd be willing to serve as a music task force member.

Appendix B

The Chapters of Life

A Six-Week Series of Worship Services

Howard Vanderwell

The following is offered as an example of the way in which inter-generational worship services can be provided. Here the worship life for a six-week period is planned to include all ages (chapters) on the journey of life. This series of service originally took place at the Hillcrest Christian Reformed Church in Hudsonville, Michigan.

The aims of these services were as follows:

- to show the congregation that each stage in life's journey is valuable and deserves attention,
- to illustrate that each stage in life's journey has its own unique challenges and needs, and
- to aid all worshipers to become more sensitive to and understanding of others who are in a chapter different from their own.

The theme song for this series of services was "O God, Your Constant Care and Love" by H. Glen Lanier. We included this song in each service because it spoke about the timelessness of God's care for us.

You will notice that most of these services were preceded by some effort to listen to those in each chapter of life. These were either small-group discussions or private conversations with key people.

Service 1

Subject and service theme: *The years of childhood contain reasons for joy and anticipation.*

Sermon title: "The Joy of Being a Child"

Scripture readings: Psalm 139:13-18 and Mark 10:13-16

Sermon digest: *The early years of life contain opportunities and joys unique to this early chapter of life, yet these are easily overlooked. The joys of being created, of growing, of discovering, of being loved, and of serving as a model of many things for adults fills this chapter with deep meaning. A healthy and vital church welcomes children, blesses them, protects them, and celebrates their presence.*

- Scripture readings were done by grade-school children.
- An anthem was a vocal ensemble of children.
- The songs of the service were carefully chosen to be child-focused and child-friendly.
- The prayer of intercession focused particularly on the needs and joys of children.

Service 2

Subject and service theme: *The chapter of adolescence is a life-shaping time.*

Sermon title: "Getting Wisdom and Understanding"

Scripture reading: Proverbs 4:1-27

Sermon digest: *All ages in the church must work together to understand the ups and downs of adolescence. This is a time of rapid growth, increased responsibilities, and intense spiritual competi-*

tion. Solomon calls his sons to "run after wisdom"—remaining teachable by reliable others, settling our relationship with God, welcoming discipline, and learning to make hard choices.

- Preparation for this service included a focus group with teens for breakfast to listen to the concerns and needs of adolescents. The sermon included a report from the focus group on what teens consider to be their biggest issues in life.
- All the readings of Scripture, the ministry of music, and the prayers were led by adolescents of the congregation.

Service 3

Subject and service theme: *The years of parenthood call us to pour ourselves into the shaping of another life and generation.*

Sermon title: "Shaping A Generation"

Scripture readings: Psalm 78:1-8 and Ephesians 6:1-4

Sermon digest: *Taking on the task of parenthood calls us to the passion of pouring ourselves into other lives so that they may be formed for full responsible adulthood. A parent's task is to tell children eternal truths, to warn them of destructive dangers, and to shape them for mature living. The Christian community welcomes and encourages those who serve in this role.*

- Preparation for this service included another focus-group discussion with young parents for the purpose of listening to their concerns, joys, and questions.
- The intercessory prayer of the service was structured in three parts:

  1. A grandmother prayed for the children of the congregation.
  2. A teenager prayed for the parents.

3. A parent prayed for families who are carrying some special pain.

- For the ministry of music the children of the church school sang some of their favorite songs.

Service 4

Subject and service theme: *Adult singleness is a valid and meaningful lifestyle.*

Sermon Title: "Singleness and Finding it Good—When We're Unmarried"

Scripture Readings: Mark 3:31-35 and John 12:1-3

Sermon Digest: *The view of singleness in the Bible is sometimes at odds with the view of many in our society. Whereas some in the church may consider singleness incomplete and inferior, the Bible speaks of its validity and integrity. A healthy church recognizes diversity, welcomes singles, encourages high-quality commitments whether people are married or single, always encourages members to value one another, and shapes its ministries for a diverse group.*

- Another focus group was scheduled with adult singles in preparation for this service. We felt it was important to listen well to the needs of this often overlooked but large group before the service was planned.
- The pastor led the pastoral prayers of the people in giving thanks and interceding for adult singles. Several singles participated as readers.

(Note: It was particularly important for this service that we were sensitive to the broad range of "singles" and the very different needs each encounters—those never married, those once married but now divorced, and those once married but now widowed.)

Service 5

Subject and service theme: *When the children are grown and gone, parents reassess their life purposes.*

Sermon title: "The Time of Reassessment"

Scripture readings: Job 42:10-17, Psalm 92:12-15, Isaiah 46:3-4, Matthew 6:25-33, 1 Corinthians 10:31

Sermon digest: *When the full responsibilities of parenthood come to a conclusion, parents face a significant adjustment that should be accompanied by a reassessment of priorities and focus. The empty nest creates a sense of loss, but also gives opportunity for time, energies, and resources once focused on the family to be directed now to other pursuits. The wise adult will be conscious of the collision between "self" and "service."*

- A focus group with empty-nesters was called together in preparation.
- All lay leaders in worship for readings and prayers were from this group.

Service 6

Subject and service theme: *The closing years of life provide a final opportunity to live our faith.*

Sermon title: "Dying Well"

Scripture readings: Genesis 25:7-11 and Genesis 49:29-33

Sermon digest: *We must be free to talk about dying, and about dying well. Biblical and personal examples of a "good death" include acceptance of it, gratitude for the years, preparation to come to closure, a freedom to express grieving, and a vital faith that trusts God's care and anticipates God's final gift of eternal glory.*

- The greatest preparation for the service came from careful listening through conversations in the course of pastoral work.
- Three men from the congregation had experienced critical illnesses in recent years in which their lives were seriously threatened. The pastor met with each of the three to talk about how each faced his mortality and death and asked each of them to give his personal testimony during this service.
- Two were able to give the testimony personally; the third was unable but allowed the pastor to read his written testimony.
- The intercessory prayers focused on the needs of those shut-in, aged, and dealing with the illnesses associated with advanced age.

Appendix C

Using This Material in Small Group Discussions

The material in this book can be used in three ways. You may read it yourself and profit (and, we hope, find your leadership shaped by it). Or you may read it yourself and then pass it on to others and suggest that they read it (thereby adding to the number of those who may profit). Or you may call a group together to both read and discuss it (in which case you will multiply the number of those who profit).

Types of Groups

If you choose to engage in a group discussion of this material, you will be providing an excellent setting for the exchange of ideas and insights that will advance the learning of all. A variety of small groups, as listed below, might discuss this book. Some groups would have a larger block of time than others; see below for suggested options.

- *An elders' meeting.* Since the board of elders is ultimately responsible for the worship life of the church in most congregations, it would be appropriate and helpful for the elders to reflect on this material together.
- *The worship committee.* If your congregation has a worship committee that meets regularly, this group would provide an excellent forum for exchanging ideas and insights.
- *A worship planning team.* Many churches have a team that meets weekly to plan worship. Its work would benefit greatly from a short group discussion each time on a portion of this material.

- *A church staff.* If your congregation has a paid ministry staff, these leaders would surely be interested in these concepts. Because each staff member carries responsibilities in her or his own area, each would have excellent insights to add to the discussion and could benefit from the ideas of others.
- *A volunteer group.* Perhaps there are others in your congregation who would be willing to commit themselves to a "book club" discussion group on the subject of intergenerational worship.

The amount of time that your group has available for this discussion will be shaped by the type of group it is. Some groups will be able to discuss only smaller sections, perhaps for 30 minutes, given an agenda of other responsibilities. Some may be able to devote an hour to the study and discussion of a specific chapter each time the members meet. In still other settings, the group may desire to set aside a day on retreat, so that the participants can talk their way through the book in a leisurely way.

Method to Follow

Careful planning and structuring will be necessary to create a setting in which the discussion can be marked by freedom, openness, and insight. Be sure you stay on course. We suggest some guidelines like these:

- A discussion leader should be designated for your group. This can be the same person at each meeting, or the leadership can be rotated among the membership.
- Decide together on the most convenient time for meetings.
- Each participant should have a copy of the book.
- Everyone should know which sections of the book will be covered in each meeting, and should agree to prepare for the meeting by reading the material assigned.

- Note the discussion questions at the end of each chapter. These can be "starters," but also give the members of your group the freedom to raise other questions.

Guidelines for Leaders

Those who are chosen to lead a group often feel that it's a daunting responsibility. True, it can be. But it can also be a rich and rewarding role. We offer the following suggestions as guidelines to help those who are placed in the leadership role.

1. Be in prayer for the members of the group and yourself, that God will give grace, insight, and courage. Pray also that God will create a deep sense of unity and bonding within the group. Your meeting should begin with prayer together. In this prayer ask for God's direction in your meeting, but also be sure to remember any personal needs that members of the group may mention.
2. Be sure that you understand the purpose of the group. At the first meeting explain it clearly so that all have the same expectations. You may wish to express it this way: "*Our purpose here is to discuss each of the sections of this book to better understand the life of the church, and to seek God's direction for our church in the matter of intergenerational worship.*"
3. Choose and arrange for the location for your meeting. Be sure the room is comfortable, large enough, but not too large. It should have an informal atmosphere.
4. Carefully read the section assigned. Review the discussion questions offered. Formulate some of your own. Avoid questions that call for a simple yes-or-no answer. Encourage several members of the group to offer their answers and insights. Receive each comment gratefully as a gift to the group. Ask other questions that may be needed to clarify the issues you are discussing.
5. Do your best to draw all members of the group into this discussion. If some are quiet and reticent, do not hesitate

from time to time to draw them out with "I'd like to hear what you think."

6. Keep the discussion on track. If it wanders too far afield onto other subjects that are not directly related to this section, remind the participants, "This is a good discussion, but I think we should return to our subject again."

7. With your tone of voice, facial expressions, and kindness to each member, try to communicate a pleasant spirit of acceptance toward all who are there.

Conserve the Learnings

It would be good to designate someone within the group to serve as a recorder who will be willing to keep notes of each meeting and at the end of the session summarize what you have discussed together. Near the end of the meeting it would be wise to ask the group for input on things such as these:

1. These are the new insights we have learned. . . .
2. These are the issues and questions we'd like to pursue further. . . .
3. These are practices/habits/methods for our congregation that need a closer look. . . .

Questions for Discussion

Notice that each chapter has suggestions for discussion by the author of the chapter. You may also want to add some of your own.

Notes

Chapter 1, A New Issue for a New Day

1. Michael Stein, *The Prosperous Retirement: Guide to the New Reality* (Boulder, Colo.: EMSTCO Press, 1998), 47.
2. Kathleen Fischer, *Winter Grace* (Nashville: Upper Room Books, 1998), 1.
3. There is no one agreed-upon way of referring to the generations or to marking the lines of division between them. One classification system includes the *matures*, born before the close of World War II; the *baby boomers*, born during the first two decades after World War II; the *gen Xers*, born generally between 1970 and 1990; and the *millenials*, born since 1990. Another common arrangement lists *builders*, born before 1947; *boomers*, born between 1947 and 1966; *busters*, born between 1967 and 1985; *bridgers*, born between 1986 and 1995; and *millennials*, born after 1995.
4. Gil Rendle, *The Multigenerational Congregation: Meeting the Leadership Challenge* (Herndon, VA: Alban Institute, 2002).
5. Craig Barnes, *Searching for Home: Spirituality for Restless Souls* (Grand Rapids: Brazos Press, 2003).
6. Jackson W. Carroll and Wade Clark Roof, *Bridging Divided Worlds: Generational Cultures in Congregations* (San Francisco: Jossey-Bass, 2002).

Chapter 2, Biblical Values to Shape the Congregation

1. See Marva Dawn, *Reaching Out without Dumbing Down: A Theology of Worship for the Turn-of-the-Century Culture* (Grand Rapids: Eerdmans, 1995), 305–307.

2. See Norma deWaal Malefyt and Howard Vanderwell, *Designing Worship Together: Models and Strategies for Worship Planning* (Herndon, VA: Alban Institute, 2005), 30–33.

Chapter 3, Worship and Faith Development

1. John Westerhoff, *Will Our Children Have Faith?* 2nd edition (Harrisburg, Pa.: Morehouse, 2000), and James Fowler, *Stages of Faith* (San Francisco: Harper & Row, 1981), have set the stage for much of the writing and thinking done about faith development in the past 25 years.
2. Fowler, *Stages of Faith*, 14.
3. A number of criticisms of this theory are discussed in Craig Dykstra and Sharon Parks, eds., *Faith Development and Fowler* (Birmingham, AL: Religious Education Press, 1986).
4. Kenneth Stokes, *Faith Is a Verb* (Mystic, CT: Twenty-Third Publications, 1989), 17.
5. Ibid., 19.
6. Fowler, *Stages of Faith*, 186.
7. Ibid., 200.
8. Walt Whitman, *Leaves of Grass* (Philadelphia: David McKay [c. 1900]; Bartleby.com, 1999, *www.bartleby.com/142* [accessed Jan. 25, 2007]).

Chapter 4, "Intergenerational" as a Way of Seeing

1. Dorothy Bass, "Congregations and the Bearing of Traditions," *American Congregations*, vol. 2, James P. Wind and James W. Lewis, eds. (Chicago: University of Chicago Press, 1994), 172.
2. Arthur Koestler, *The Ghost in the Machine* (New York: Macmillan, 1967), 55.
3. Daniel S. Schechter, *Synagogue Boards: A Sacred Trust* (New York: UAHC Press, 2000), 77–83.

4. Gil Rendle, *The Multigenerational Congregation: Meeting the Leadership Challenge* (Herndon, VA: Alban Institute, 2002).
5. Ronald Heifetz, *Leadership without Easy Answers* (Cambridge: Belknap Press, 1994).

Chapter 5, Fostering an Intergenerational Culture

1. Hugh Koops, "Children's Church," *The Reformed Journal*, Dec. 1967, 5.
2. "Grandma," "Voices—Children's Church—Yes or No?," *The Banner*, Nov. 12, 1976, 22.
3. Helen W. Hoffman, "Voices—Defends Children's Church," *The Banner*, Jan. 14, 1977, 24.
4. Koops, "Children's Church."
5. See George Brown, Jr., "Making Room for Children," *Religious Education*, vol. 68, no. 3 (May–June 1973).
6. See CRC Publications Report, *Agenda for Synod: Christian Reformed Church of North America* (Grand Rapids: CRC Publications, n.d.), 39. The details of this approach are presented in Sonya Stewart and Jerome Berryman, *Young Children and Worship* (Louisville: Westminster John Knox, 1990).
7. See Sofia Cavalletti, *The Religious Potential of the Child: The Description of an Experience with Children from Ages Three to Six,* trans. Patricia M. Coulter and Julie M. Coulter (New York/Ramsey, N.J.: Paulist Press, 1979), 1983.
8. Janet Soskice, *Metaphor and Religious Language* (Oxford: Clarendon Press/New York: Oxford University Press, 1985), 57–58; quoted in William P. Brown, *Seeing the Psalms: A Theology of Metaphor* (Louisville: Westminster John Knox, 2002).

Chapter 6, The Power of Telling a Story

1. Eugene Peterson, *The Message* (Colorado Springs: NavPress, 2002), 105.

2. The script of the play *Sioux Center Sudan* may be downloaded at *www.nwciowa.edu/barker/plays*

3. John D. Witvliet, *Worship Seeking Understanding* (Grand Rapids: Baker Academic, 2003), 31. Read chapter 1, including the footnotes.

4. Ibid., 31–32.

5. Ibid., 32.

6. Ibid., 36.

7. Karen, my wife and colleague, told me she was teaching a high school girls' Sunday school class on the bad women of the Bible. They came to Delilah, and Karen said, "Just listen while I read you the story." She read the entire Samson story from Judges 13–16. When she finished, one of the girls said, "I've never heard that whole story before." None of the girls had. Why do you suppose that is? Most of these girls had been raised in the church. Something's going on regarding our stories. Could it be that we live in a culture that greatly prizes story (perhaps even more than the church), and the culture's stories have attracted us away from our own?

8. See "Testimony" by Thomas Hoyt, Jr., in the book edited by Dorothy C. Bass, *Practicing Our Faith* (San Francisco: Jossey-Bass, 1997); Thomas G. Long's *Testimony* (San Francisco: Jossey-Bass, 2004); and Fred Craddock's *Craddock Stories,* Mike Graves and Richard F. Ward, eds. (St. Louis, Mo.: Chalice Press, 2001).

9. See Thomas E. Boomershine, *Story Journey* (Nashville: Abingdon, 1988). Check out the work of the Network of Biblical Storytellers online at *www.nobs.org*.

10. Donald Miller says, "It makes you wonder whether we can even get to the truth of our theology unless it is presented in the sort of methodology Scripture uses. It makes you wonder if all our time spent making lists would be better spent painting or writing or singing or learning to speak stories. Sometimes I feel as though the church has a kind of pity for Scripture, always having to come behind it and explain everything" (Donald Miller, *Searching for God Knows What* [Nashville: Nelson Books, 2004], 217).

11. Tom Boogaart says, "Our quiet times are too quiet!"

12. Lin Sexton leads a multigenerational drama team at First Baptist Church in Modesto, California. Read more about this ministry in the September 2006 issue of *Worship Leader* magazine.

13. You can read the scripts of the Northwestern College drama team Old Testament narratives at *www.nwciowa.edu/barkerplays* and see clips at *www.nwciowa.edu/worshipdrama*

14. Written by Roger Schrock, who gave me permission to share it.

15. This sort of celebration won't work with every single story. Some stories bring us to face the world's suffering, and the correct response is lament.

Chapter 7, The Power of Preaching to All Ages

1. Augustine of Hippo, *On Christian Teaching: Book Four* (Oxford, England/New York: Oxford University Press, 1997).

2. Barbara Brown Taylor, *The Preaching Life* (Cambridge/Boston: Cowley Publications, 1993).

3. Eugene Peterson, *Subversive Spirituality* (Grand Rapids: Eerdmans, 1994). I also would like to note that while I did not directly quote Eugene Peterson's wonderful book *Eat This Book: A Conversation in the Art of Spiritual Reading*, it is everywhere being echoed in the section titled "The Doors Swings In: The Process of Discovering What We Are to Learn."

4. Karl Barth, *Church Dogmatics: vol.1, The Doctrine of the Word of God* (Edinburgh: T&T Clark, 1936).

5. Abraham Heschel, *God in Search of Man* (New York: Farrar, Straus & Giroux, 1955).

6. Augustine of Hippo, *On Christian Teaching: Book Four.*

7. The word is *LALEO* and it appears several times in the Acts, most notably in the Acts 11:19–20.

8. O. Wesley Allen, Jr., *The Homiletic of All Believers: A Conversational Approach* (Louisville: Westminster John Knox, 2005).

9. Augustine of Hippo, *On Christian Teaching.*

10. Richard Lischer, *Open Secrets: A Spiritual Journey through a Country Church* (New York: Doubleday, 2001).

11. Walter Brueggeman, *Finally Comes the Poet: Daring Speech for Proclamation* (Minneapolis: Fortress Press, 1989).

12. L. Frank Baum, *The Wizard of Oz;* adapted by Frank Gabrielson, with music and lyrics of the screen version by Harold Arlen and E. Y. Harburg (St. Louis, Mo.: Municipal Theatre Association, 1978).

Chapter 8, One Congregation's Story

1. Jacob Eppinga, *A Century of Grace* (Grand Rapids: LaGrave Avenue CRC, 1987).

2. Books read were Dorothy Bass and Dan Richter, *Way to Live* (Nashville: Upper Room Books, 2002); Carolyn Brown, *Forbid Them Not* (Nashville: Abingdon, 1994); Colleen Carroll Campbell, *The New Faithful: Why Young Adults Are Embracing Orthodox Christianity* (Chicago: Loyola Press, 2002); Dan Kimball, *The Emerging Church: Vintage Christianity for New Generations* (Grand Rapids: Zondervan, 2003); Carol Lytch, *Choosing Church: What Makes a Difference for Teens* (Louisville: Westminster John Knox, 2004); Debra Dean Murphy, *Teaching That Transforms: Worship as the Heart of Christian Education* (Grand Rapids: Brazos Press, 2004); Gwen Kennedy Neville, *Learning the Liturgy* (New York: Seabury, 1978); Jane Rogers Vann, *Gathered Before God: Worship Centered Church Renewal* (Louisville: Westminster John Knox, 2004).

3. Consultants: Carolyn Brown, minister of education in several Presbyterian churches and author of *Forbid Them Not*; Darwin Glassford, professor of church education at Calvin Theological Seminary, Grand Rapids, Mich.; Carol Lytch, director of Lilly Endowments at Louisville Presbyterian Seminary and author of *Choosing Church*; Ed Seeley, youth specialist at Calvin College and Calvin Theological Seminary, Grand Rapids, Mich.; Jane Rogers Vann, profes-

sor of church education at Union Theological Seminary, Richmond, Va.; John Witvliet, director of the Calvin Institute of Christian Worship, Calvin College, Grand Rapids, Mich.

4. Jane Vann in an interview in November 2005.

5. Ed Seeley in an adult education presentation at LaGrave Avenue CRC in November 2005.

6. Carol Lytch in an interview in December 2005

7. Carolyn Brown in an adult-education presentation at La-Grave Avenue CRC in November 2005.

Chapter 9, Intergenerational Connectors in Worship

1. Craig Dykstra, *Growing in the Life of Faith: Education and Christian Practice* (Louisville: Geneva Press, 1999), 126.

2. Karen Wilk, ed., *Together All God's People: Integrating Children and Youth into the Life of the Church* (Grand Rapids: Faith Alive Christian Resources, 2005), 36.

3. Carolyn Brown, *Gateways to Worship* (Nashville: Abingdon, 1989), 103.

4. *The Worship Sourcebook* (Grand Rapids: Calvin Institute of Christian Worship, Faith Alive Christian Resources, and Baker Books, 2004), 100.

5. John D. Witvliet, "Vertical Habits—Worship and Our Faith Vocabulary," Calvin Institute of Christian Worship Web site (*www.calvinv.edu/worship/habits/*), a lecture, April 13, 2007.

6. Debbie Hough and Mary E. Speedy, *Children in the Sanctuary Study Guide* (Louisville: Church Leader Support, Presbyterian Church U.S.A., 2002), 11.

7. Brown, *Gateways to Worship*, 49.

8. Michael Perry, *The Dramatized Old Testament*, 2 vols. (Grand Rapids: Baker Publishing Group, 1995).

9. Lynnae Keeley, quoted in Howard Vanderwell and Norma deWaal Malefyt, "Worship that is Friendly to Children," part 2, Calvin Institute of Worship Web site.

10. John D. Witvliet, ed., "Teaching Some Basic Aspects of Worship," *A Child Shall Lead: Children in Worship* (Garland, Texas: Choristers Guild, 1999), 45.

11. David Vroege, "Prayers for the Christian Year for Adults and Children," *A Child Shall Lead: Children in Worship,* John D. Witvliet, ed. (Garland Texas: Choristers Guild, 1999), 86.

Chapter 10, Worship Planning in a Church of All Ages

1. See deWaal Malefyt and Vanderwell, *Designing Worship Together,* in which we discuss this in more detail on pages 40–49.

2. A sample "Volunteer Resource Bank Survey" is also provided in *Designing Worship Together,* 30–31, or can be found in appendix A.

3. Debra Rienstra, *So Much More: An Invitation to Christian Spirituality* (San Francisco: Jossey-Bass, A Wiley Imprint, 2005), 165.

4. John D. Witvliet, "Vertical Habits—Worship and Our Faith Vocabulary," Calvin Institute of Christian Worship, Calvin College, April 13, 2007.

Suggested Resources

General Writings

Barnes, M. Craig. *Searching for Home: Spirituality for Restless Souls*. Grand Rapids: Brazos Press, 2003.

This volume explores the spiritual journey of Americans as a longing for home. Settlers, exiles, and nomads are all expressing their search for home in different ways.

Carroll, Jackson W., and Wade Clark Roof. *Bridging Divided Worlds: Generational Cultures in Congregations*. San Francisco: Jossey-Bass, 2002.

Two authors explore a variety of congregations in southern California and North Carolina to learn of the ways in which religious communities bridge generational divides.

Dawn, Marva. *Reaching Out without Dumbing Down*. Grand Rapids: Eerdmans, 1995.

A classic publication that names a concern which many have and addresses it theologically, practically, and understandably. The church must be open to all while retaining its spiritual and theological integrity.

deWaal Malefyt, Norma, and Howard Vanderwell. *Designing Worship Together: Models and Strategies for Worship Planning*. Herndon, Va.: Alban Institute, 2005.

On the basis of their work together, the authors explore how a congregation can benefit from collaborative efforts in its worship planning that take into consideration the needs of all worshipers.

Fowler, James. *Stages of Faith: The Psychology of Human Development and the Quest for Meaning.* San Francisco: Harper & Row, 1981.

Drawing on development psychology, the author analyzes the process of human development, especially through the early years of life.

Freudenberg, Ben, with Rick Lawrence. *Family Friendly Church.* Loveland, Colo: Group Publishing, 1998.

This volume offers principles for the inclusion of all ages of the family in church and explains how this aim necessitates the partnership of home and church efforts.

Freudenberg, Ben, et al. *Family Friendly Ideas Your Church Can Do.* Loveland, Colo.: Group Publishing, 1998.

A ton of practical ideas (for learning, worshiping, and serving) designed to engage parents and children together in their worship life.

Groome, Thomas H. *Sharing Faith: A Comprehensive Approach to Religious Education and Pastoral Ministry.* San Francisco: Harper, 1991, 337–378.

These pages offer an honest discussion of the inherent educational aspect of liturgy.

Hines, John M. *By Water and the Spirit: New Concepts of Baptism, Confirmation, and Communion.* New York: Seabury, 1973.

An effort to view children as members of the church who can understand and participate in the sacraments.

Kimball, Dan. *The Emerging Church: Vintage Christianity for New Generations.* Grand Rapids: Zondervan, 2003.

The "deconstruction" of postmodern ministry and the reconstruction of vintage Christianity in the emerging church.

McIntosh, Garry L. *One Church, Four Generations: Understanding and Reaching All Ages in Your Church*. Grand Rapids: Baker Book House, 2002.

An examination of four generations in a congregation and an analysis of how they stay connected with each other.

Murphy, Debra Dean. *Teaching That Transforms: Worship as the Heart of Christian Education*. Grand Rapids: Brazos Press, 2004.

Worship and religious education have a formative relationship together. Healthy religious education leads to healthy worship.

Rendle, Gilbert R. *The Multigenerational Congregation: Meeting the Leadership Challenge*. Herndon, Va.: Alban Institute, 2002.

Some of the differences experienced in a congregation are based on members' tenure or length of membership rather than on age. The author focuses on how to understand and communicate with each other.

Reformed Worship 76, June 2005. Grand Rapids: CRC Publications.

A theme issue on intergenerational worship. Available online at *www.reformedworship.org*.

Townsend, Michael J. *Companion to the Lectionary: Worshipping God Together,* vol. 6. London: Epworth Press, 1996.

Materials for intergenerational worship covering Years A and B of the Revised Common Lectionary.

Vann, Jane Rogers. *Gathered Before God: Worship Centered Church Renewal*. Louisville: Westminster John Knox, 2004.

For this resource the author studied 10 vibrant churches; her findings show that worship is vital to the renewal of congregational life.

White, James W. *Intergenerational Religious Education.*
Birmingham, Ala.: Religious Education Press, 1988.

> An extensive presentation of models, theory, and prescription
> of learning designed for the entire faith community.

Witvliet, John D., and Emily R. Brink, eds. *The Worship
Sourcebook.* Grand Rapids: Calvin Institute of Christian
Worship, Faith Alive Christian Resources, and Baker Books,
2004.

> An extensive volume of resources for worship services,
> including prayers, readings, litanies, teaching sections,
> and liturgy suggestions. Part 1 organizes all the resources
> according to the elements of the worship service. Part 2
> organizes all resources according to the central themes of the
> Christian faith and the Christian Year.

Concerning Children and Youth

Apostolos-Cappadona, Diane, ed. *The Sacred Play of Children.*
New York: Seabury, 1983.

> An ecumenical collection of essays providing foundations for
> how to construct liturgies and celebrate the Eucharist with
> children, based on the Directory for Masses with Children.

Ban, Arline J. *Children's Time in Worship.* Valley Forge, Pa.:
Judson, 1981.

> An argument for including children in the worshiping
> community in ways that respect their perspectives and
> abilities.

Boling, Ruth L. *Come Worship With Me: A Journey through the
Church Year.* Louisville: Geneva Press, 2001.

> A book for children and for use with children, which takes
> a journey through the main events of the church year and
> explains them understandably.

Boling, Ruth L., Lauren J. Muzzy, and Laurie A Vance. *A Children's Guide to Worship*. Louisville: Geneva Press. 1997.

A tool to aid parents and teachers in explaining the elements of worship to children.

Brown, Carolyn, *Forbid Them Not*. Nashville: Abingdon, 1994.

Based on the Revised Common Lectionary, year C, it provides a year of resources that will aid the participation of children in public worship.

————. *Gateways to Worship: A Year of Worship Experience for Young Children*. Nashville: Abingdon, 1989.

Designed for those who teach children in the church setting of worship. After describing five movements within worship (praise, confession, proclamation, petition, and dedication), Brown provides guides and resources for the entire year.

————. *You Can Preach to the Kids, Too! Designing Sermons for Adults and Children*. Nashville: Abingdon, 1997.

Ideas and suggestions for making the "real sermon" child-friendly as well as adult-friendly.

Buchanan, Aimee Wallis, Bill Buchanan, and Jodi Martin. *Making Worship Real: A Resource for Youth and Their Leaders*. Louisville: Geneva Press, 2001.

Explains the significance of each part of the worship in Presbyterian (U.S.A.) and Reformed congregations and includes activities designed to help youth think creatively about worship.

Carroll, Colleen. *The New Faithful: Why Young Adults are Embracing Orthodox Christianity*. Chicago: Loyola Press, 2002.

An analysis of the search of young adults for meaning and discussion of how the issues of worship, faith communities, and fellowship are integral to their search.

Castleman, Robbie. *Parenting in the Pew: Guiding Your Children into the Joy of Worship*. Downers Grove, Ill.: InterVarsity Press, 2002.

> Encouragement and instruction for parents so that they can effectively prepare their children to worship meaningfully.

Chapman, Kathleen. *Teaching Kids Authentic Worship: How to Keep Them Close to God for Life*. Grand Rapids: Baker Books, 2003.

> Motivation and instruction for teaching children about worship: what it is, how to do it, and why we worship.

Dawn, Marva. *Is It A Lost Cause? Having the Heart of God for the Church's Children*. Grand Rapids: Eerdmans, 1997.

> Writing from her passion for the youth of the church, the author exposes the church's neglect of children and youth, and points to directions for healthy ministry.

Fairless, Caroline S. *Children at Worship: Congregations in Bloom*. New York: Church Publishing, 2000.

> Though not written from the standpoint of a typical congregation, these ideas about the inclusion of children will stretch you and make you think.

Funk, Virgil C., ed. *Children, Liturgy, and Music*. Washington, D.C.: Pastoral Press, 1990.

> Scholarly essays on getting children genuinely involved in the liturgy.

Halmo, Joan. *Celebrating the Church Year with Young Children*. Collegeville, Minn.: Liturgical Press, 1988.

> Halmo focuses on the liturgical year and offers families ways to encourage and include young children's participation in worship, particularly at home.

Henderson, Dorothy. *45 Ways to Involve Children in Worship: Ideas for Worship Planners, Worship Leaders, and Parents.* North York, Ontario: Presbyterian Church in Canada, 1997.

> As the title indicates, here is a helpful list of ideas to work from.

Hough, Debbie, and Mary Emery Speedy. *Children in the Sanctuary: Involving Children Fully in the Worship Life of a Congregation,* with a study guide. Louisville: Church Leader Support, Presbyterian Church U.S.A., 2002.

> An examination of the meaning of worship and the opportunities for children to participate in, lead, and plan worship.

Juengst, Sara Covin, *Sharing Faith With Children: Rethinking the Children's Sermon.* Louisville: Westminster John Knox, 1994.

> This book includes practical, well founded advice on approaches to cultivate meaningful children's sermons, and pitfalls to avoid.

Keeley, Robert. *Helping Our Children Grow in Faith: Nurturing the Spiritual Development of Kids.* Grand Rapids: Baker Book House, 2008.

> The author pleads for a three-dimensional faith: of the head, the heart, and the spirit. He expands on how the church community aids this search and development.

Lytch, Carol, *Choosing Church: What Makes a Difference for Teens.* Louisville: Westminster John Knox, 2004.

> An examination of the religious life of teenagers and how the church must minister to them.

Ng, David, and Virginia Thomas. *Children in the Worshiping Community.* Atlanta: John Knox, 1981.

> One of the early and classic expressions of the theology and philosophy of children worshiping.

Reformed Worship 12. Summer 1989. Grand Rapids: CRC Publications.

> A theme issue on children in worship (available online at *www.reformedworship.org).*

Reformed Worship 36. June 1995. Grand Rapids: CRC Publications.

> A second theme issue on children in worship (available online at *www.reformedworship.org).*

Sandell, Elizabeth. *Including Children in Worship: A Planning Guide for Congregations.* Minneapolis: Augsburg Fortress, 1991.

> A planning guide that includes lots of "how to" ideas for committees.

Schalk, Carl. *First Person Singular: Reflections on Worship, Liturgy, and Children.* St. Louis: MorningStar Publishers, 1998.

> A collection of personal reflections by a Lutheran church musician and scholar on the participation of all ages of children in worship.

Sneller, Kathy. "How To . . . Encourage the Children in Your Congregation to Worship—Ideas for Worship Planners (1)." *Reformed Worship 55.* Grand Rapids: CRC Publications, 44 (available online at *www.reformedworship.org).*

————. "How To Encourage Your Children to Worship—Tips for Parents (2)." *Reformed Worship 57.* Grand Rapids: CRC Publications, 44 (available online at *www.reformedworship.org).*

> In this pair of articles, Sneller gives ideas for worship planners and parents to promote the thoughtful participation of children in worship.

Stewart, Sonja M., and Jerome Berryman. *Young Children and Worship.* Louisville: Westminster John Knox, 1989.

> A Montessori approach to preparing children for worship, including a structured series of worship experiences for

younger children that aims to develop reverence and quiet participation skills.

Stonehouse, Catherine. *Joining Children on the Spiritual Journey: Nurturing a Life of Faith,* Grand Rapids: Baker Book House, 1998.

This book presents the Christian education of children—how the spiritual life of a child develops and how caring parents and teachers can enhance this development.

Sytsma, Mary, and Jane Vogel. *Sunday Morning Live: How and Why We Worship.* Grand Rapids: Faith Alive Christian Resources, 2003.

A course of study for youth that explores the basis of worship and helps teens understand the elements of worship.

Wilk, Karen J., compiler. *Together All God's People—Integrating Children and Youth into the Life of Your Church.* Grand Rapids: Faith Alive Christian Resources, 2005.

A guidebook to aid the congregation in determining how well it is currently integrating children and youth into every area of church life.

Vanderwell, Howard. "Kids of the Kingdom—Four Services with a Focus on Children," *Reformed Worship 36.* Grand Rapids: CRC Publications, 11 (available online at *www. reformedworship.org*).

An outline of four worship services, built around the stories of four children in the Bible, designed for a multigenerational congregation.

Vander Meer, Harriet, and Betsy Steele Halstead, *Rings, Kings, and Butterflies: Lessons on Christian Symbols for Children* with CD-ROM. Minneapolis: Augsburg Fortress, 2006.

A helpful resource for teachers, worship leaders, and parents who want to help children learn about Christian symbols and the seasons of the church year, including downloadable versions of art and helpful handouts.

Westerhoff, John. *Bringing Up Our Children in the Christian Faith*. Minneapolis: Winston Press, 1980.

A classic exposition of the nurturing process for faith development in children in which the Christian community partners with parents.

———. *Will Our Children Have Faith?*, 2nd edition. Harrisburg, Pa.: Morehouse, 2000.

An update and partner to Westerhoff's previous volume to point out new considerations in the nurturing process because of the diminution of the Christian faith in society.

Witvliet, John, ed. *A Child Shall Lead: Children in Worship*. Garland, Texas: Chorister's Guild; and Grand Rapids: Calvin Institute of Christian Worship, 1999.

A collection of essays that provides a wide-ranging sourcebook for Christian educators, musicians, and clergy. It is packed with practical ideas and thoughtful descriptions for increasing the role of children in worship.

Contributors

TAKA ASHIDA is pastor of Shin-Urayasu Reformed Church in Japan, Tokyo, Japan.

J. GEORGE AUPPERLEE is chaplain at Holland Home, Grand Rapids, Michigan.

JEFF BARKER is professor of theatre and speech at Northwestern College in Orange City, Iowa.

BRUCE BENEDICT is worship ministries director at Redeemer Presbyterian Church in Indianapolis, Indiana.

TIMOTHY BROWN is the Henry Bast professor of preaching at Western Theological Seminary, Holland, Michigan.

ANNAMAE BUSH is worship planner at Church of the Servant Christian Reformed Church, Grand Rapids, Michigan.

KAREN DEMOL is professor of music at Dordt College in Sioux Center, Iowa

NORMA DEWAAL MALEFYT is resource development specialist in congregational song at Calvin Institute of Christian Worship and instructor in organ at Calvin College, Grand Rapids, Michigan.

MARY ELDER is lay leader of Fredericktown United Methodist Church, Fredericktown, Ohio.

RANDY ENGLE is pastor of North Hills Christian Reformed Church in Troy, Michigan.

BETH ANN GAEDE is a writer and editor for the Alban Institute.

DARWIN GLASSFORD is associate professor of church education at Calvin Theological Seminary, Grand Rapids, Michigan.

BETHANY KEELEY is a graduate student in speech communication at the University of Georgia, Athens, Georgia.

LAURA KEELEY is a curriculum writer and children's ministry director in Holland, Michigan.

ROBERT J. KEELEY is professor of education and worship planner at Calvin College, Grand Rapids, Michigan.

YOUNG KIM is assistant professor of history at Calvin College, Grand Rapids, Michigan, and lay worship leader at Cornerstone Christian Reformed Church, Ann Arbor, Michigan.

STAN MAST is minister of preaching at LaGrave Avenue Christian Reformed Church in Grand Rapids, Michigan.

ELEAZAR MERRIWEATHER is pastor of St. Luke African Methodist Episcopal Zion Church in Grand Rapids, Michigan.

ROBERT NORDLING is co-director of Christian formation and orchestra conductor at Calvin College in Grand Rapids, Michigan.

GIL RENDLE is a senior consultant at the Leadership Institute of the Texas Methodist Foundation, Austin, Texas, and an independent consultant to congregational systems.

CAROL ROTTMAN is a writer and teacher and a member of Eastern Avenue Christian Reformed Church in Grand Rapids, Michigan.

EDWARD SEELY is a former adjunct professor of education at Calvin Theological Seminary and Calvin College, and research associate for the Calvin Institute of Christian Worship, Grand Rapids, Michigan.

JIMMY SETIAWAN is director of worship for Jakarta Baptist Church, Jakarta, Indonesia.

MARK STEPHENSON is director of disability concerns for the Christian Reformed Church, Grand Rapids, Michigan.

CATHY ROBBS TURNER is director of education at Christ United Methodist Church, Chattanooga, Tennessee.

HOWARD VANDERWELL is resource development specialist for pastoral leadership at Calvin Institute of Christian Worship and adjunct professor of worship at Calvin Theological Seminary, Grand Rapids, Michigan.

ANNE ZAKI is resource development specialist for global resources at Calvin Institute of Christian Worship, Grand Rapids, Michigan.

JAN ZUIDEMA is director of music ministries at Second Christian Reformed Church, Grand Haven, Michigan.